Stepping into Darkness

by Kathleen Tedsen
& Beverlee Rydel

THUNDER BAY
— P R E S S —

Stepping Into Darkness
by Kathleen Tedsen

Published by
Thunder Bay Press
West Branch, MI 48661

First Printing October 2017

ISBN: 978-1-933272-63-4

Cover Design: Kathleen R. Tedsen
Front Cover Photo: Kathleen R. Tedsen
Back Cover Photo: Julie Welch

Printed in the United States of America

hauntedtravelsmi.com

**Wisdom tells me I am nothing. Love tells me I am everything.
And between the two my life flows.**

~ Nisargadatta Maharaj

Other Titles by Kathleen Tedsen and Beverlee Rydel

Haunted Travels of Michigan

Haunted Travels of Michigan, Volume II

Haunted Travels of Michigan, Volume III: Spirits Rising

Coming Up With *Stepping Into Darkness*...

It was shortly after my sister Bev's cancer diagnosis that we began the concept of this book. We wanted it to be different than our *Haunted Travels of Michigan* series but weren't certain of its direction.

It was a hot summer's day. My sister and I decided to spend it at our "off-site" meeting room, which was Bev's pool. While doing our float-thing, we talked on and off about the book.

When pool time was over, we had decided it would be a collection of true stories that seemed to have a logical conclusion but ended with a twist that took the reader into an area that was unexplained. The title, however, remained elusive.

After finishing our "meeting", Bev went to take a shower while I sat outside thinking about the book's name. For some reason, Stepping Into Darkness just popped into my head. A few minutes later Bev came out and, before I could say a word, said, "Hey! I have a name. What do you think of Stepping Into Darkness?"

Bev passed away before completing *Stepping Into Darkness*. It took a couple of years, but I have now finished the work we started.

This is our last project together. We hope you enjoy it.

Table of Contents

Chapter 1   Eloise Psychiatric Hospital   1

Chapter 2   The Night Visitor   15

Chapter 3   Spirit Painter   23

Chapter 4   Direct Voice Medium   43

Chapter 5   House of Funerals   61

Chapter 6   Eternal Retribution of the Sauk   77

Chapter 7   Lost Boy of Mackinac Island   85

Chapter 8   Murder House   99

Chapter 9   The Fate of Sister Mary Janina   111

Chapter 10   The Last Goodbye   145

Post Script: *A Tribute to Beverlee J. Rydel*   165

Eloise Psychiatric Hospital

Westland, MI

Eloise Psychiatric Hospital often appears on the Top 10 list of Michigan's Most Haunted. This always makes me wonder. All patient buildings were torn down years ago. Only the administrative office and powerhouse remain. It seems these buildings would be the least likely to have paranormal activity. Adding to that, controlled paranormal investigations are not permitted. There was one ghost hunt conducted for a small TV station a number of years back. That, however, turned up nothing remarkable other than dust floating around an empty room.

Yet, there it is on Top 10 lists. Why? Possibly the name "psychiatric hospital" or "insane asylum" just automatically gives people that creepy feeling that makes them think the place must be running rampant with ghosts of the insane. I don't know about that. I do, however, know what happened to me as a young college student at Eloise in the mid-1970's. An experience that would forever impact my life. An experience more unsettling than any fabled ghost stories.

Before I share what happened, however, let me take you through a bit of Eloise's past. It has quite a fascinating history.

Photo opposite: Eloise today (Malena Fryar)

1

The land where Eloise stands was the former location of the Black Horse Tavern, a stagecoach stop, pub, and overnight lodging for travelers up to the early 1830's. Around 1839, it became a poorhouse. The old log cabin

Wayne County House, ca. 1913 (Stanislas Keenan)

became the keeper's quarters and a frame building was erected to house the poor. Its first residents came from a badly rundown poorhouse in Hamtramck, Michigan. Back then, Nankin Township was a wilderness and many residents staying at the decayed Hamtramck facility refused to go. Only 35 agreed and the Third County Poor House was established. It expanded not long after. A cook house was built behind the log cabin to serve the residents and keeper's family. The facility continued to grow with an increasing number of residents. Around 1894, a post office was opened on the grounds. They named the post office after the Post Master's daughter, Eloise Dickerson Davock. It was then the Third County Poor House became known as the Eloise County House and Asylum.

In the 19th century, the reason people were committed is shocking. For example, a husband could commit his wife for not obeying him or for being lazy. Other reasons for commitment included postpartum depression, promiscuity or an immoral life, asthma and even political excitement. Because of the loose standards for commitment, the populations at insane asylums skyrocketed.

Treatment methods for patients were often more torturous than helpful. Residents were neglected. Conditions were overcrowded. In 1909, estimators went to the Eloise County House and Asylum; what they found was highlighted in a June 7, 1909 article in the Detroit Free Press, "Sorrowful Sights seen at Eloise by the Estimators." According to the estimators, the asylum was "filled with wrecks of humanity."

Not long after, Eloise received additional funding to upgrade its facility. From there it expanded and continued to grow. It added a full-service medical care facility and became known as a state-of-the-art facility. Eloise was one of the first to use x-rays for diagnostic purposes and first in the state to offer kidney dialysis and use of barium as part of a comprehensive cancer treatment. It was also one of the first to offer open-air treatment for tuberculosis. Additionally, Eloise adopted state-of-the-art procedures and meth-ods for psychiatric pa-tients, implementing music and TV therapy into its treatment program. There was also liberal use of elec-troshock and insulin shock therapy as well as lobotomies.

At its peak, there were 75 buildings housing an estimated 10,000 residents. Then came the Great Depression and its decline began. Psychiatric care ended in 1979. The general

Bridget (Biddy) Hughes, Wayne County Asylum's first psychiatric patient 1841-1895 (Stanislas Keenan)

hospital closed in 1984. Almost all of the 75 buildings were demolished by the mid-1980's. Today, only the administrative building and power-house remain standing.

As might be expected, there were many deaths over the decades. When families or friends did not claim remains of the deceased, the asylum unceremoniously buried them. The Eloise cemetery, off limits to visitors, holds approximately 7,100 of those forgotten souls. Graves are marked only by numbered blocks. Recently, more unmarked graves have been discovered. That site is currently under excavation but they estimate the area likely contains more than 3,000 remains.

My story begins in 1974. I was a young college student attending a first year psychology class. One of the projects our professor gave us was to go to a psychiatric facility and become friendly with a patient.

The project required establishing communication with a patient authorized by the hospital's medical team. We were not there to give guidance, of course. We had no authority or qualifications for that. We were there just to make friends and observe changes, if any, over the course of their treatment. At the end of the semester, we were each to write a paper detailing our observations. Eloise Psychiatric Hospital was the closest facility near me. That was the location I chose.

I was extremely shy back then and had no idea what to expect. I mean, for heaven's sake, I had a difficult time talking to a mentally competent person. The thought of trying to make idle conversation with someone not fully competent was more than daunting. I admit not sleeping the night before my first visit to Eloise.

The impact of the asylum on my first approach was overwhelming. The buildings were huge, imposing, intimidating. As I turned my car into the main entrance, I glanced up at the rows of windows. The upper floors were all dark, seemingly vacant except for one. There I saw the ghostly image of a face watch my car approach. It was no ghost, of course, just the blank stare of someone in the building. I could not tell if it was a man or woman, but one thing was certain, the figure stood perfectly still, unmoving, and remained so after I pulled the car into a parking spot and walked into the main office.

Once inside, I introduced myself to the woman at the reception desk. She took me to a small conference room where a couple of other college students were sitting. I didn't know any of them but felt some relief knowing I wasn't the only one involved in this project.

We didn't have much time for chitchat. Just moments after I sat down, a middle-aged woman entered the room. She gave us a few instructions and handed us a pass to wear whenever we visited. Little information was given about our assigned case. We were only told the individuals were not dangerous to themselves or others. With that she took us on a tour of some of the buildings. Here is where the real education began.

The first thing I noticed was how dark and depressing the hallways were. Paint was chipped in several places and I spotted stains of unknown origin along several walls. Although the

The origin of Eloise Asylum's name: Little Eloise Devok, daughter of the postmaster (Stanislas Keenan)

floor was clean and shiny, I could see scuff marks and hairline cracks that were indelibly sealed beneath the shiny coating. Vague light filtered into dreary hallways from rooms on either side. Patients were slowly wandering back and forth. Many seemed oblivious to their surroundings. They

5

shuffled forward only briefly glancing up, obviously uninterested in our small group.

My stomach clenched when I saw a nearly naked man lying on the floor. I thought for a moment he was dead until his foot moved and I realized he was just sleeping. That was unsettling. A woman in a loose-fitting flowered dress stood unmoving, leaning face forward against a wall. OK. That was also unsettling.

Our small group lightly stepped around the near naked man and the statue-like woman. I glanced over at one of the other students. He was a short, heavyset guy with thick, dark hair. He gave me a half-smile as his eyebrows raised and his eyes rolled. Oh boy. I was praying the patient I was assigned wouldn't be like the naked man or the catatonic woman. Really, at that point in my life, I was certain I could not make idle conversation with someone who was either unable to respond or naked.

We were led into a larger room that looked like a gathering room or social room. There were a number of inmates sitting or standing around. Some were talking to each other. Others were sitting at small tables playing checkers or cards. It was a brighter room although the old, scarred windows resisted the full impact of the bright, sunny day.

Our guide took us to several other locations, including the main dining hall and commissary. Truthfully, I don't recall much of what I saw there. Overall, however, the place looked old, worn, and more than a little dreary. There was a heavy, intense atmosphere that gave me a sense of doom. Not a great place, I thought, for troubled patients to feel better.

A distinct smell came from a few areas that caused my stomach to roll and required breathing through my mouth. The location that I do recall was the high security area. It looked like solitary confinement at a prison. Solid doors were closed tight. Only a small opening on each door was visible. We were not permitted to go into this area but I looked down the hallway. I heard quiet sobs coming from behind one of the doors and saw fingers emerge from the opening of another. The supervisor told us this area was used for patients who were most aggressive and considered a danger to themselves or others. I felt great sadness for whoever was locked behind those doors. What a hideous existence. Their minds unable to think clearly, were they filled with anger and rage or just confused and frightened? I didn't know but it seemed horrible.

Eventually we were led to another gathering room, this one slightly smaller than the first. Here we were introduced to the patients who would be our "subject" for the semester. That's when I first met Mark.

I can't tell you how relieved I was to see him. He was young, perhaps just a few years older than me, and seemed quite normal. He wore

Psychiatric Dorm, Men's Building, ca. 1913 (Stanislas Keenan)

loose fitting jeans and a light blue shirt that was buttoned all the way to the top. Mark was tall and slender with longish hair that was slicked back with some type of hair product. He had a gentle-looking face.

He smiled, shook my hand and said, "Nice to meet you, Kathleen." Very formal. I wasn't used to being addressed in such a way and thought it was great.

We sat down and started what most would consider a normal conversation. The conversation centered on our favorite music, movies, the school I was going to, and what we liked to do for fun. He had been at Eloise for just a short time and was an in-out patient. That meant he stayed at Eloise but was able to go out during the day to work.

I asked what brought him here. He shrugged and shook his head. He enjoyed illegal substances too much and when he took them would go a little nuts. Cocaine was his drug of choice though he was open to anything that got him high.

Mark felt he shouldn't be at Eloise. It was a mistake. Then he added that he sometimes got depressed and a few times had tried to end his life. I looked down and saw scars over each wrist. They were pinkish in color and slightly raised. He knew I saw them and let the finger of one hand run across the scar of the other.

Mark told me that he had sat in a bathtub full of water and cut his wrists. He didn't want to get his parents' house dirty. I didn't say anything but mentally wondered why someone so young would want to end his life. As though reading my mind, he looked at me intently and said that sometimes life just sucked. He didn't want to do it anymore. He didn't want to live.

Mark was going to have group therapy a few times a week. According to him, they were trying to get into his head and figure out what was wrong. However, he felt there was nothing wrong except for the fact that life sucked. Mark told me no one could understand that sometimes death is better. He laughed. They wanted him to dry out and get sober. Then to get a handle on his bipolar condition and extreme mood swings, they wanted to give him more drugs. How ironic, he thought. They wanted him to quit taking drugs so they could give him more drugs.

The time I spent with Mark on that first visit went very quickly. I was fascinated by his situation and excited at the opportunity of talking with him again. I returned a week later. Things had changed. Not for the better. I met him in the larger gathering room. He was sitting by himself in a corner. Dark circles under his eyes told me he wasn't sleeping well. His hands fidgeted. It might be signs of withdrawal. I had done some research on cocaine addiction withdrawal and knew that mood swings were expected. These mood swings could last for weeks and months. Not a good thing for a young man who was already having extreme mood swings. I had also read that sleep problems were common and that many addicts experienced nightmares during withdrawal. If that was true, Mark looked like he was on track with what I'd read.

He wasn't in a good mood and didn't especially want to talk to me. He was silent but listened as I went on about anything I could think of…the weather, my instructor, movies I wanted to see.

At one point he abruptly cut me off saying he'd lost his job, was broke, then asked if I'd buy him a Coke and candy. I agreed and we went to the commissary. He took a seat while I paid what I thought was a ridiculous amount of money for a Coke, candy and small bag of potato chips. It didn't take long for him to scarf down the candy. He started talking as he munched on the chips.

He thought the place was a "shit hole." He couldn't sleep. The beds were awful and the rooms smelled. The doctors were idiots and he hated group therapy. According to him, the whole thing was "fucking useless." He also didn't like the fact that he was my school experiment. I told him it wasn't like that but if he'd changed his mind I would let the supervisor know and was certain someone else could be found. He shook his head no and said it was OK.

While the first meeting went quickly, this one dragged. He said very little. He wasn't in the mood for idle chatter and didn't want to talk. There was something going on inside his head. That was obvious. I said goodbye and stood to leave. It looked for a moment like he wanted to tell me something but changed his mind.

It wasn't until the third meeting that he told me about the recurring nightmares. He would dream that things came into his room at night. Dark, awful things. He either couldn't or wouldn't describe them to me. He only said it scared the crap out of him and when he'd wake up he couldn't get back to sleep. Were they the continued symptoms of withdrawal? I didn't know. It wasn't my call. I asked if he'd told the doctors about this and what they'd said. He didn't answer, just shrugged and rolled his eyes.

One of the patients sat on a bench not far from us and had overheard our conversation. He was an older man, maybe in his 60's or early 70's. To be honest, he looked a little loopy. My impression was that he'd been at Eloise a long time. Anyway, I remember him pointing a finger at Mark and telling him they weren't nightmares he was having. "The things you're seeing are real. They're everywhere. Everywhere!" His voice raising at the end. The guy said that these things would mess with your brain—just like the doctors did. He pulled out a large cross from under his worn shirt and held it out to Mark. He found faith in the Lord and it was his faith that kept him safe from the dark things. I dismissed his words as those of a man living in a world of paranoia and delusion. He also upset me because I could see the old guy's words were having an impact on Mark. So, before his rant could continue, I asked Mark to go for a walk with me.

I returned the fourth week. The shadows surrounding his eyes seemed even darker and it looked as if he had lost some weight. I asked him how he was doing. He stared at me and said, "What do you think?" No response was needed. The nightmares were continuing and getting worse. More frightening. They were no longer part of his dreams but real. He now saw them when he was fully awake. They would linger near patients and near him. He didn't only see them at night, he could sometimes see them in the day. They weren't as inky black as they were at night, but if you looked carefully, you could see their faded images moving down hallways, in the dining area, public rooms.

Mark's hands pushed through his hair as he grew more animated, agitated. When he first came to Eloise he didn't think he was crazy. However, Mark knew what he was telling me sounded crazy and was quite fearful he *was* going crazy.

Mark looked at me, the edge of desperation in his eyes.

He laughed then, reached in his shirt and pulled out a small cross. "See, I even got one of these. Don't know if it'll help but it sure can't hurt. Right?"

I asked if he saw any shapes now. His eyes darted around for a few seconds then he shook his head. "Not now."

The doctors had given him some new medication. He thought maybe they had made it worse. He'd lost his appetite and wanted out of Eloise. Mark had asked his parents to help him. He swore if they didn't get him out he would do something drastic.

I remembered what Mark had told me during our first meeting, "Sometimes death is better." I became worried and told him not to do something foolish. Not to hurt himself.

For the first time, he was making me nervous. His eyes avoided mine and he would only briefly glance in my direction. I was surprised at how his personality had changed in just a few weeks. Addiction and withdrawal can do terrible things to people. Is this what was going on here?

At one point he smiled and told me he was going to make a hell of a good subject for my class paper. "I'll bet you get an A because of me." Then he asked what I was going to say about him in the report. I told him I didn't know yet. I wanted to see him get better. Be happy. He laughed again, looked away and said, "Yeah. Whatever."

Before I left that day, I contacted the supervisor saying I was concerned about Mark. She said she'd look into it and not to worry. I did worry about him, of course. In fact, I thought about him all weekend and was eager to see him the next week.

To my great distress, a day before the next visit my professor pulled me aside after class and told me I wouldn't be going back to Eloise. Mark was no longer available for the study. I was told not to contact Eloise or Mark.

What had happened? Had Mark gotten worse? Perhaps his parents had gotten him out? Was it something I did wrong? Then I wondered if he'd done something drastic, as he had said. Had Mark ended his life? My instructor assured me the reason had nothing to do with me but, rather, Mark. He had no idea what had happened to Mark or at least that's what he told me.

I completed my report up to the end of our last session. Just as Mark had predicted, I got an A on the paper.

I've always wondered what happened to him. I didn't know his last name. He didn't know mine. There was no way to trace him down. However, he has become part of my past in a strange, disconnected way. A story that, for the first time, I'm sharing with you. Were the nightmares Mark experienced symptoms of his drug withdrawal and the older man's visions his own troubled, mental disease? Or were there really dark things at Eloise that wandered the halls unseen and into the dreams of tortured patients?

I don't know if Eloise is haunted or was haunted, but I do know some of its patients were.

The Night Visitor

It was a dark time. My mother had died. This intelligent, loving woman who had always been there for my sister and me...my mentor, muse, and strongest supporter was gone. The ability to believe in myself and love others were the greatest gifts she gave me.

After a long, truly horrible illness, I prayed she was now at peace. Although I was personally quite lost. The thought of her love and support no longer being a part of my life was impossible to consider.

My sister, Bev, my husband, Chris, and I supported each other as we moved through the profoundly difficult period following her death. At the end of each day, I found myself mentally and physically exhausted and would quickly drop off into a coma-like, dreamless sleep until the alarm rang the next morning. That is, until one night.

It was February, a couple of weeks after mother's passing. I awoke, not sure what had caused me to stir. The digital numbers of the clock read 3:35 a.m. The time of my mother's death. Chris' slow, deep breathing next to me confirmed he was soundly asleep.

I lay there unmoving, my eyes adjusting to the room's darkness. A faint glow from the nightlight in the corner

Artwork opposite: Typical representation of the Hat Man (author)

cleared my vision just enough to make out the colorless shapes of objects in the room, including a single sock on the floor. Big deal. It would stay there for now. I didn't have the motivation to get up and put it away.

I glanced at the partially opened door. It was just as I'd left it. The house was silent. Everything was in order. I slowly closed my eyes hoping sleep would resume. It didn't. I sighed deeply, knowing slumber was not in my immediate future.

That's when something imperceptibly changed. A heavy, silent stillness settled around me. My eyes moved to the doorway again. It was still partially opened just as I'd left it but I sensed there was now something there. Hovering, unseen on the other side.

Without a sound he came in. A man. His features were indistinguishable but I could clearly see his outline. He wore a wide-brimmed hat that partly obscured his face and a long, flowing coat almost like a cape. He was hunched slightly forward, his movement slow and smooth, floating rather than walking across the floor. He didn't glance my way nor did he move directly toward me. Rather, the intruder made his way across the room on an angle toward the foot of our bed.

What I did next made absolutely no sense. I didn't reach over to warn Chris. I didn't even make a sound. I simply closed my eyes and waited for death. Even stranger, I wasn't afraid. My thoughts, at least to my own mind, were clear. If he killed us, it would be okay. There was nothing I could do to stop it. At that moment, I accepted the inevitability of death and waited.

My eyes remained closed for several long seconds. Nothing happened. When I opened them again, he was gone. The atmosphere in the room had returned to normal. Chris remained sound asleep beside me and that stupid sock was still on the floor.

I sat up in bed and ran fingers through my hair. What had just happened? I got up, grabbed the sock and threw it in the hamper then decided to look around the house. Nothing. Not a sound or a sign that anything was out of place.

It had snowed that evening and I looked outside to see if any footprints were visible. Nothing. Whatever had been there, if anything had actually been there, was gone. I lay back down in bed and questioned the reality of what I had seen. Eventually I drifted off to sleep.

I awoke later that morning. There was no logical explanation for what happened that night other than it was a dream. It was just my troubled subconscious mind symbolically projecting and accepting the inevitability of death. Not just my mother's death but death as a part of all life. Yet still, as much as I knew it was a dream, it had seemed so real.

Life for Bev, Chris and I continued. Nearly a year passed. The shadow man did not return and I eventually forgot about the dream.

For over 15 years Bev and I had authored a book series called the *Michigan Vacation Guide.* It was a bestseller in Michigan for a number of years and made it to the Secretary of State's "Read Michigan" list acknowledging its significance to Michigan travel and tourism. My mother was a huge part of its success.

In fact, she was a key part of the book's inception. It may not have happened without her help. Near the end, even when quite ill, she would sit at the kitchen table until the wee hours of the morning proofreading what Bev and I had written, making comments and offering suggestions. After her death, we lost interest and decided not to continue the series.

Bev and I went into a temporary limbo of sorts. My sister began focusing more heavily on her Human Resource consulting work and I on various writing, print and advertising projects.

Perhaps it was fate that brought Chris, Bev and me to the beautiful Whitney Restaurant in Detroit, Michigan one evening. At the time, we were completely unaware of its haunted reputation. In fact, ghosts and paranormal phenomena were not a part of our life or even interest at that time. We were there simply for the elegant, beautiful atmosphere and its reputation for exceptional food.

After dinner, we decided to explore the restaurant. Bev had brought her camera, wanting to take photographs of its stunning architectural design. The next day we were looking at her photos and came across the photo. When I say the photo, I'm talking about a strange picture taken down a hallway on the second floor. In the far lower left-hand corner of the picture, unnoticed initially, was an unusual shape. It looked a bit like a tornado on its side with a small hole in the center.

I sent the photo off to an acquaintance of ours who, at the time, worked as a photographic forensic analyst. At first he thought it was dust but days later messaged saying he did not believe it was. The only information he

was able to provide was that it was something moving at a rather high rate of speed. Other than that, he was unable to provide an explanation. That photograph was the catalyst for our journey into the paranormal and the *Haunted Travels of Michigan* book series.

In 2007, we attended our first paranormal convention in Philadelphia. The convention included an investigation at Eastern State Penitentiary.

This was the strange photo taken at the Whitney Restaurant.

The investigation of the penitentiary was uneventful and, truthfully, many of the presentations left us yawning. But there was one speaker I clearly remember. It was Rosemary Ellen Guiley, a well-known author of books on spirituality and the paranormal. Her topic was a phenomenon called "Shadow People".

Over a period of time, she had interviewed hundreds of people who had experienced visions of a shadow phantom. In most cases, they appeared in their bedrooms between the hours of 2 a.m. and 5 a.m. As she continued the story, I could feel the hair begin to rise on the back of my neck as my hands slowly tightened around the arms of the chair.

Each person would wake in the early morning hours to see a solid, dark shadow figure in his or her room. Sometimes it would be standing at the foot of their bed staring at them. Other times they'd see it wander in from their bedroom door or closet. It was inky-black and, though detailed features were never visible, it was clearly a man.

The Hat Man, contributions from Andrew* (top left), Denise Coyle (top right), Sheryl* (bottom left) and Dani Demink (bottom right). *Last name withheld on request

She began showing pictures drawn by those she'd interviewed. I looked, fixed gaze, with mixed feelings of surprise and fear. The expression on my face must have revealed my inner feelings because Chris leaned over and whispered, "Are you okay?"

I looked him, shook my head. "My dream," I whispered.

He didn't understand. "That's him," I explained, pointing to the roughly drawn images appearing on the screen. "The dream I had after mom's death. That's him!"

There on the large screen were roughly etched drawings, each similar, consistent. It was the dark figure of a man wearing a wide brimmed hat and a flowing cape-like coat. Exactly what I had seen after my mother's death. I had never met these people yet they had seen exactly what I had seen.

Chris looked at the screen, then back at me. Bev leaned forward and silently mouthed the words, "What's up?" Chris explained while I just continued to stare at the screen.

That's when I learned the vision I had seen had a name. It was called "The Hat Man," one of a handful of shadowy silhouettes incorporating the Shadow People phenomena. According to Rosemary, some people are terrified of this entity. Others, like me, had no fear whatsoever.

Rosemary believed the experience of seeing Shadow People is very widespread. Many around the world have had this experience.

Who are they? Why do they go to the foot of the bed? Why the hat? No one really has an answer. Rosemary thinks these shadowy images may be a Djinn, an entity from another dimension that exists unseen on this earth. Perhaps it is a guardian from the other side.

Yet others claim it is a harbinger of change or emotional upheaval – divorce, death, illness, or other major life-changing events. Rosemary believed that in cases of emotional turmoil, the very energy we project from this strong emotion might draw them to us. Some suspect shadow entities are a throw off of our own consciousness. Certainly, the emotional turmoil and subconscious projection could have applied to me in the days that followed my mother's death.

There are, of course, physiological and psychological conditions that can account for reported experiences of these shadowy shapes. Yet, with that said, what I saw that evening at 3:35 a.m., the time of my mother's death, was incredibly real. I believe I was completely awake. In spite of that, there may still have been a momentary projection of my subconscious. Whether this was imagined or real I will likely never know in this life—this existence.

It has been over ten years since my mother's death. Over that period of time I have experienced profound loss. My life, my entire existence, has changed and been challenged. I lost my devoted husband, my soul mate, from an unexpected heart attack three years after my mother's passing. Two years after that my incredible sister, my life-long best friend and comrade in paranormal research, was diagnosed with advanced stage cancer. Three years later, after a courageous fight, she was gone.

In spite of these tragic events, I have not seen the Hat Man again. Why did he come that evening?

The night I saw the Hat Man was the night I accepted death. To me he was the messenger of death, the harbinger of profound grief and life-changing loss.

I have seen the Hat Man. I hope you never do.

The Spirit Painter

Bay City, MI

It is said a spirit painter is an extremely rare person whose works of art are guided by the unseen hands of the spirit world. The images they create will reveal the secrets of the other side, the place of heaven, a place where there is no time and everything is known. Those same unseen hands will guide the spirit painter in foretelling the future of the earth and its inhabitants.

This is the story of a spirit painter and what the spirits revealed through her hands. What they foretold and when it will happen is unknown because in their world time does not exist. They only know it will happen.

She was born Flora Mae Spore in Portsmouth, Michigan, 1878. She was named after her grandmother, Flora, but went by the name of Marian. Marian looked much younger than her years would suggest and, as time progressed, her year of birth would change from 1878 to 1892.

Diminutive in size, she had tawny-red hair and deep brown eyes. Marian was attractive, charismatic and was said to have the "It Factor". There was just something about her that was irresistible, indefinable, making her appealing in the eyes of many.

Photo opposite: Flora Mae Spore, 1899 (University of Michigan yearbook)

23

Marian's father, Melvin, worked as a school teacher, later moving his career to the railroad business when they moved to Bay City, Michigan. He wasn't an especially doting father. To soften his hardness was Marian's mother, Helen. She was a kind, loving, very nurturing woman. Marian adored her.

Melvin and Helen had five children. The oldest was Albertajayne (Bertie), next came Marian, followed by Norman, James, and their baby, Sarabelle (called Belle). Sadly, little Norman died at the age of one from brain fever (encephalitis).

They lived in a modest home on a quiet street a few blocks from downtown Bay City. The Spores were just an average family growing up in a middle-class neighborhood in the late 19th century. No one would have guessed back then, not even Marian, where the future would take her.

Marian often said that she'd had dreams and premonitions of things to come as far back as she could remember. These dreams and premonitions would often come true. In her youth, however, it was a secret, one she shared with no one but her mother and immediate family.

Her mother would smile and nod her head. Helen's British ancestors had come from northern Scotland. The Highlands, Helen said, was an area in Scotland where its people were known for their abilities to commune with the spirits and foretell the future. In fact, Helen's own ancestors had strong psychic attributes and that gift was passed down to Marian. Helen encouraged her daughter to embrace the gift and not fear it.

Although Marian had dreams and premonitions, she refused to believe they came from spirits or ghosts. The very idea of spirits or ghosts terrified her. She could not sleep if she thought they were creeping into her mind while she slept. It was dreadful to think about. So she denied it.

Helen loved all of her children dearly but she shared a very special bond with Marian. Perhaps it was the fact that Marian had that special gift of the Scots. The two were inseparable. Helen was Marian's chief supporter, mentor and best friend.

As Marian would often recall, the two had established a wonderful, close telepathy. They would often duplicate the actions of each other without knowing it, including sending out similar letters or duplicating orders, speaking the same words at the same time, and many other smaller, personal things.

After completing high school in 1895, Marian decided on a career in dentistry, and was accepted into the University of Michigan's program. This was certainly an unusual career for a woman in the late 19th century. In fact, there were no female dentists in all of Bay County at the time.

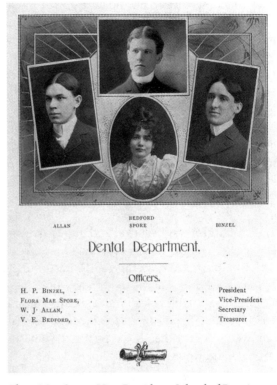

Dental Department.

Officers.

H. P. Binzel, ... President
Flora Mae Spore, ... Vice-President
W. J. Allan, ... Secretary
V. E. Bedford, ... Treasurer

Flora Mae Spore, Vice-President. School of Dentistry (University of Michigan 1899 Yearbook)

Bertie, Marian's sister, was just a year older. She was also attending the University of Michigan. Bertie was happy that Marian would be joining her in campus life and they enjoyed many good times together.

1896 started as a great year. Both Marian and her older sister, Bertie, returned to the University of Michigan to begin the new semester.

As the semester progressed, however, Bertie believed she had either acquired a little cold or had developed an allergy of some sort. She started coughing. At first it was barely noticeable but progressively got worse.

When she started coughing up blood and became weaker, they took her to the doctor. To everyone's horror, Bertie was diagnosed with tuberculosis.

Back then, there was really no cure for the disease, with survival rates extremely low. The only treatment was isolation, a good diet, exercise and pure, open air.

The entire family was frantic. Bertie was terrified. She did not want to die! Helen was devastated but remained strong and positive for Bertie's sake.

The doctor recommended a brand new, state-of-the-art tuberculosis hospital called Mount Sanitas–Boulder Colorado Sanitarium. The sanitarium was founded by well-known Battle Creek, Michigan native, Dr. John Harvey Kellogg (founder of the Kellogg Cereal Company) and was run by the Seventh Day Adventist Church.

The sanitarium was beautiful and quite grand compared to the others. Daily exercise was encouraged, including hikes in the mountains. An orchestra played to calm the guests. Beautiful paintings were found on the ceilings, and a view of the mountains could be seen from every window. The facility also offered a unique dietary program. Through a progressive series of steps all poisonous food (caffeine, meat, white bread, etc.) were removed from the diet. It was believed wholesome foods made the body stronger and would drive out tuberculosis.

They also offered alternative treatments like hydrotherapy tonic baths to heal the lungs and body. And the special waters used for hydrotherapy came from the pure waters found at the base of Mt. Sanitas. It simply seemed to offer everything possible to cure Bertie.

Helen, Melvin and Bertie saw a sliver of hope at Mt. Sanitas. Unfortunately, it was very, very expensive. Helen and Melvin would figure the money out later. What was important was to get Bertie into that facility. They did.

In spite of their efforts and the expense, by late April Bertie's condition had greatly worsened. She kept fighting but finally couldn't fight any more. She died in early May of 1896.

It was dreadful, heart-breaking. None of the treatments or diet helped. Bertie was gone.

Now Marian took over responsibilities as the oldest sibling. It was her responsibility to care for her younger siblings as well as support her mother and father during this incredibly difficult time. Melvin, tough soul that he was, carried on. Helen and Marian drew even closer.

Marian graduated from the University of Michigan's College of Dentistry in 1899. A standout in her studies, she became Vice President of the College of Dentistry and was respected for her knowledge and abilities.

Marian set up practice in Bay City and became the county's first female dentist. Initially, she established an office and laboratory in the Phoenix Block, located on the corner of Washington and Center Avenues. It wasn't long before her expertise in the fabrication of inlays, crowns and bridges became well known. To this day, she is considered a pioneer in the field of periodontal dentistry.

The years passed. Life for Marian and the Spore family continued. Marian did not marry, rarely dated and only had a few close friends. In spite of that, she was content with her life, career and independence. She had her mother, sister and brother, and her work.

Then May 30, 1919 came. Helen died. That's when it all changed.

Helen's death seemed to tear Marian's heart into shreds and she fell into profound despair. Of course, Marian expected Helen's inevitable death. Not from her psychic ability but simply the reality of Helen's failing heart. Indeed, she saw death approach as the energy and joy faded from her mother's eyes.

In spite of knowing the inevitable, the fact that she was now gone was overwhelming. Nothing in her life was important, not even her own existence. She lost interest in everything, including her dental practice. Although she didn't act hysterical, inside Marian was collapsing. At one point she even contemplated suicide.

Her greatest concern was to know if her mother, wherever she was, was happy. In life, Helen had frequently told her if it were possible to return to her after death she would. So Marian waited for a message from Helen.

As the hours and days passed into weeks, she grew more anxious, morose. She missed her mother desperately. Why hadn't she sent her some sign? Although Marian had once been terrified of ghosts, that fear had vanished knowing the ghost coming back would be that of her beloved mother.

A thought came to Marian. Perhaps she had missed the signs her mother was giving. She became vigilant—watching, waiting. Marian didn't know exactly what to expect. She was so inexperienced. She just hoped her mother would provide some obvious signal to let her daughter know she was okay. Three months passed and nothing came.

Marian was angry. Although Marian was not a traditionally religious person, she wondered how the laws of the universe could be so cruel as to not allow two people who were so close in life to be permanently, irrevocably separated after physical body death.

She was determined to find a way to communicate with her mother. Whatever that method was, it would not involve mediums. Both Marian and her mother had always held mediums in contempt, believing they were pretenders. With that not being a consideration, Marian had to find a way by herself. She would trust no one else.

Approximately three months after her mother's passing, a stepping-stone was presented to her. A friend passed on an article written by the famous author of the Sherlock Holmes book series, Arthur Conan Doyle. In that article, he confirmed the ability to communicate with those who had passed through a method called automatic writing and use of something called a Ouija board. At the time she didn't know what that was but would find out.

She spent an entire day going to the stores in Bay City and, eventually, found the Ouija board in a toy store. She brought it home but then had second thoughts. It was, after all, a toy! The term "toy" was plainly written on the cover. It seemed almost disrespectful to communicate with her mother with a toy. She put the board away and forgot about it.

Then, one day, she witnessed a terrible accident in downtown Bay City. An old man was accidently run over by a car in front of her. It was a dreadful sight and the poor man died instantly.

A few weeks later she read an article in the paper saying that a couple of well-known residents of Saginaw had been playing Ouija while vacationing on Lake Huron. They knew nothing of the accident or the death of the old man.

What the article claimed happened during the Ouija session was, to Marian's mind, stunning. The words formed by the Ouija's planchette were from an old man who was frightened and confused. He did not know what had happened to him or where he was. As the Ouija spelled out, he awakened and found he was no longer old but young and healthy again. The last words spelled out were - pretty street - car accident - water. It then spelled out the man's name.

It all made sense to Marian. The location where the man died was an attractive section of town right by the water. The man's name spelled out by the Ouija turned out to be the correct name. In fact, it led the authorities to his home in West Bay City and notification of family.

Marian sat back. It was a toy but perhaps it was more than that. What did she have to lose?

The directions said you needed two or more people for it to work. She decided to ask her father to join her in the first session. He somewhat reluctantly agreed. According to Marian, the moment the two of them placed hands on the planchette it started to move.

Each accused the other of directing the planchette. Both swore they were not. For the next few minutes it moved aimlessly around the board as if familiarizing itself with placement of letters. At some point, the letters started forming words and short sentences.

The messages were from her mother. According to Marian, what was spelled out were of a highly personal nature and confirmed to both her and her father that it was her mother.

She held a second session. This time her sister, Belle, joined her. Again the planchette responded once both women placed their hands on it. But this time, the movement was sluggish, slow.

At one point Belle became chilled and got up to get a sweater. That's when something unexpected happened. The planchette began to move under Marian's hands alone. Both women gasped in surprise and watched as the planchette spelled out more words moving faster with each second.

This time the message came from her sister, Bertie. It said that Bertie had been there for their mother during the transition and all was well. It continued to spell out messages that confirmed to the two sisters that their deceased sister was speaking with them.

The true significance of this session is that Marian did not need anyone but herself to work the board. This would be the beginning of Marian's education and a future that would open many revelations into the spirit world.

In the days that followed, Marian frequently found herself on the board spending long periods communicating with her mother or Bertie. It was at one session, however, when the messages began to change. They became mysterious and frightening. A few gave warnings and other messages were chilling.

As the messages continued to grow darker, Marian pulled her hands from the planchette, unsure if she should continue. This was no longer her mother or sister. Who was it?

At the time she was very inexperienced and had no idea what she was dealing with, what to expect or how to proceed. She put the board away, fearful of what might come through if she continued.

A time came, however, when she needed to speak to her mother again and hesitantly pulled the board out. Helen did return. Marian was so happy to hear from her. As quickly as Helen came, however, she retreated, and the dark messages came through again more frightening than before. It left her with a terrible, impending sense of doom.

Yet, still, she continued and the negative messages became interspersed with positive ones. Sometimes the messages were accurate and other times hurtful, suggesting she do something that, when she followed through, ended up embarrassing or humiliating her.

Marian was suspicious of these dark, unsettling messages and was not sure where they came from. She wanted to believe they were meant simply to intimidate her. However, it was possible these messages from the dark ones could be dangerous. As sessions continued, more positive, uplifting messages came through. The positive messaged were from the good souls.

The good souls encouraged her to continue communicating. When the negative entities realized they were no longer upsetting her, they would go away. So Marian continued. She learned how to turn the negative forces away and accept only the good during her sessions.

As Marian came to learn, in that realm time does not exist. So, if the good souls predicted something would happen in the future, they could not give a specific date as to when it will happen. It could be the next day, next year, or many years in advance.

Marian quickly began identifying the good souls by their extensive use of symbolism and broad terms. She was mesmerized by what they said. Their vision was endless, beyond human comprehension. She soon discovered there were not just a few that surrounded her but many.

Eventually they (the good souls) suggested Marian leave the Quija board and try automatic writing. It would be faster. A friend bought her a planchette that had an area to place a pencil. Initially, she produced a series of unintelligible lines and shapes. That turned to words and the words to sentences. The words and sentences were so clear as to be certain what they were telling her. What they shared about life on earth and what it was like on the other side was, to Marian's inexperienced mind, mesmerizing.

A soul or spirit on earth animates the body it possesses. On earth the soul is challenged to do good, bad, demonstrate charity or greed. It is destined

to experience happiness and profound sadness. Once the body is done, the soul leaves all behind but takes with it the knowledge it gained on earth.

If the soul led a selfless life, if they truly loved and gave to others, the new existence would be that of pure love. Whatever pain or illness you had on earth is gone in the realm. You will be healthy and strong. If you were insecure, sad, fearful or lonely that, too, was gone. You will know security, and contentment. You will feel and will be loved.

Souls coming to the realm enter as adults. Even if a child died when they transitioned, they arrive fully mature as if they had lived out a full life on earth. Someone very aged will transition to a much earlier age.

At the highest level, the colors are vibrant. These souls remembered earth life and the beauty of nature. The very color of the trees, oceans and sky were more vivid in this realm than on earth.

The spirits told her even the worst of the worst on earth would come to the realm. The murderers, sadists, and evil-doers came. They would not enter at the highest level but would be guided and taught the way by souls who have. In this way they would continue to grow until they entered the area of perfect love and happiness.

It is in this highest level that the soul would be reunited with their soul mates. Those were people on earth who had shared an unbreakable bond, a glorious love. A soul mate could be a spouse, friend, or family member. Here they would remain for eternity.

The good souls further explained that when a soul entered the highest state, they kept very busy. It was a type of work but not the kind known on earth. Rather, it's work that brings the soul greatest fulfillment and joy. Perhaps it's helping new souls transition without fear or guiding those who need help to achieve the highest level, or even learning to play an instrument. They worked on many things.

The good souls shared much more. Marian, like a sponge, absorbed it all. Each writing session, lasting hours, drew her further into their world and helped her understand the glorious existence in this unknown realm. A place that those on earth, even if seen, may not fully understand. A place not meant to be understood until we leave this physical world.

It was the summer of 1921 when Marian decided to leave her dental practice. She needed to get away from everything that was familiar. Perhaps leave her grief behind as well and find more time to devote to her new form of communication.

At the time her brother, James, was the Lieutenant Governor of Guam. He invited her to come stay with him and his family. Marian accepted the offer and would soon find herself in a new life far away from the small town she had always known. During this time, Marian frequently traveled between Guam and the Philippines. She became entranced by the peaceful beauty found in both locations and the people were accepting and kind. It was during this time Marian's communication with the spirits would turn into something phenomenal.

One day, while communicating with her mother, she was asked if she would like to draw pretty images. Marian knew nothing about drawing. The truth was, she was never especially interested in paintings or artistry of any kind. Neither was her mother. It seemed an unusual request from Helen. Then Marian considered the likely possibility her mother had learned to do that on the other side.

The thought of drawing with the writing planchette sounded unique. Marian agreed. She placed her hands lightly on the planchette. It began to move.

At first the lines were meaningless squiggles. Eventually they began turning into rudimentary shapes and then discernable images. If Marian believed this was a new form of communicating with her mother, she was wrong. It was much more than that.

During one sitting, Helen came forward to tell Marian it wasn't she that moved her hand but another. Helen had met a spirit on the other side who had been an artist while on earth. It was this spirit who guided

Marian's hand. Helen thought it might take away some of her daughter's sadness if she learned to draw and the artist had agreed to help.

Drawing with the planchette continued. The images became clearer and

more detailed. At one point she discarded the device, allowing the spirit to guide her hand freely. The drawings became more refined.

It became clear to her several months into this phase that there was more than just one spirit artist working with her. The style of art she created was so different.

One of the spirits gave the name of Dore. Initially, Marian did not know the name. She would later learn of the well-known 19th century French artist, Gustave Dore, who had passed in 1883.

Marian Spore Bush at her easel (Marian S. Bush)

Another spirit painter, the one that led her hand in drawing landscapes and flowers, was a woman. She gave the name Della Robbia. Again, Marian had no idea who that was. Later in life, during a visit to the Metropolitan Museum of Art she would be drawn into a room to find a beautiful sculpture. The name of the artist who did that work was Luca della Robbia, a 15th century artist.

This was a new form of adventure for Marian. She felt excited, energized and for the first time since her mother died, very happy. She never knew what would be revealed with each new drawing. Some were mysterious and bizarre while others calming and beautiful.

Some days she wanted to question these spirit helpers. They told her that if she asked for or questioned anything, they would retreat. If she needed to know something, they would tell her but she was not to interject her wishes or wants on them. She learned to simply accept what they offered. She moved from writing pencils to crayons and then to colored pencils. They would tell her what colors and telepathically instruct her where to place and move her hand. She tried not to think too much during the creative process and simply allow the spirit to guide her hand. With time her artwork grew, changing from pencil to oil paints.

Upon returning to America, her work continued. The spirits shared images depicting what was seen in their realm. One showed a strange looking vessel that was the image of a ship bringing souls of the deceased to their glorious new life. Another revealed an other-worldly landscape with exotic flowers and greenery. The colors were brilliant and vivid.

Her paintings were being noticed by scholars of fine arts and some of the most sophisticated galleries in New York and London. Marian's work was different, a standout among current artists of the period.

Critics described the paintings as bohemian, primitively artistic, powerful, and mystical. Colors were strong with oils layered in thick peaks and valleys, almost like a sculpture. She would use a nail file or jack knife to press in or carve out areas of oil, allowing them to stand several inches from the canvas. Some appeared almost three dimensional. The size of her paintings varied but most canvases were five feet by three and one-half feet.

In 1922, Marian moved to New York, rented a studio, and lived on 144 W. 16th Street, near the artsy community of Greenwich Village. She was soon being exhibited at the finest galleries. Her name was spoken in elite circles. She became a socialite, a celebrity, and was known as the spirit painter.

In 1924 the great magician and escape artist, Harry Houdini, came to one of Marian's exhibits. Houdini was not just well-known for magic but also his skepticism of spiritualists. He was sometimes referred to as the anti-spiritualist. Although he very much wanted to believe in the afterlife, he didn't believe the nonsense spiritualists claimed when communicating with the dead. He investigated many so-called spiritualists and took pride in identifying and revealing their tricks and fakery.

He wasn't exactly sure what to think of Marian Spore or her work. She didn't claim to be a spiritualist. In fact, she detested use of the word in connection with what she did.

He came to one of her exhibits expecting to dismiss her as merely another artist with an interesting imagination. After meeting her and seeing her work, he left feeling somewhat different. In an article written in the New York Sun newspaper, Houdini was quoted as saying, "It is a great exhibition. I am certain of Miss Spore's honesty. I have never excluded the possibility of supernatural intervention from my belief. I have been engaged in the exposure of criminal fakers… there is no question of that here. Miss Spore has something beautiful and is conveying it to her fellow men."[1]

By the mid-1920's, Marian Spore's paintings were rapidly selling. Her wealth was growing with her sky-rocketing popularity.

It was around 1927 when Marian was traveling through a section of New York called the Bowery. It was a slum district. Along with the dime store clothing shops were brothels, grungy dance halls and dive bars. Crime was very high. She saw homeless men, women and children sleeping in doorways or aimlessly walking the streets. Conditions were dreadful.

Once she saw the wretched condition that existed here she knew she had to do something. Money was not the problem. She had plenty of it, certainly more than she would ever use or need. She decided to start a breadline and soup kitchen. It would be one of the first of its kind.

A few days a week, Marian would literally stand on the sidewalk handing out meal tickets, clothing, spectacles, false teeth, even wheelchairs. Thousands of dollars came out of her pockets every month. As bad as things were, as needy as folks were in the Bowery, it was about to get worse.

October 29, 1929. The stock market crashed, banks collapsed. People's savings vanished in a moment. Companies closed their doors or laid off most of their employees. Instantly the world was thrown into something that would be known as the Great Depression. Work was nowhere to be found and unemployment rates soared. The financial situation for those in the Bowery fell into even deeper despair.

---

1 Wilcox, Uthai Vincent. "Ghosts Guide Her Hand When She Paints." *Boston Sunday Post*, 30 Oct. 1927.

People waiting in Marian's breadline now spanned blocks. It was more than she could handle. She started taking donations and asking for volunteers as she expanded locations.

She opened up other breadlines throughout the district. Volunteers from all walks of life came to help. The people she was helping were grateful and her reputation and name changed from that of spirit painter to Lady Bountiful of the Bowery.

One of the volunteers who came to offer help was a man by the name of Irving T. Bush. He was born in Ridgeway, Michigan. His parents came to Brooklyn when he was a child and in New York he remained.

Irving was one of New York's wealthiest businessmen. He owned the Bush Terminal Company in New York and The Bush House in London, a multi-million dollar warehouse operation. He also dabbled in a few other business ventures.

Irving had heard of Marian's spirit paintings, of course. He was curious about them and her. He also admired her rather selfless, philanthropic efforts and decided to volunteer at one of her breadlines. That is where they met.

The attraction was instant. For the first time in Marian's 50 years of life, she was in love. There was no denying it. Marian had thought that emotion was unreachable for her, yet now she found exactly that in the eyes of Irving T. Bush.

Irving was also clearly smitten. He had never met anyone like her. This woman with the bobbed red hair and deep brown eyes was smart, empathetic, mysterious, a little wild, and beautiful. She definitely had "It!"

He was married to his second wife at the time and immediately filed for divorce. On June 9, 1930, exactly one hour after his divorce was final, Irving married Marian in Reno, Nevada. She became Marian Spore Bush. Irving swore he had never met a woman like Marian and pledged his eternal love. He swore to never leave her…and he never did.

Although her spirit paintings did not stop after the marriage, they did change. It was in the early 1930's when her typical bright colors changed to darker, monochromatic tones. Many were stark black and white.

Some of the paintings depicted disturbing demon-like creatures, misery and death. Marian, like others, also found the paintings disturbing but could not stop what she was driven to create. Images seemed to foretell world events and conditions.

Among the new series of paintings were those of war. A war that had not yet happened but when it began would cover the world. At the time, things were beginning to brew in Europe. However, the extent of trouble had not yet reached the shores of America. Marian's spirits sent warnings through her paintings of what was to come.

Spirit predictions may have first begun in September 1933. That September, a New York paper published an interview conducted with Marian. In that interview, Marian shared a message from her spirits. Something dreadful was coming to the world. They mentioned a small island would be a target and that the attack would be by land and air. They told her it would be the most terrible war the world has ever known.

When Pearl Harbor was attacked and America entered World War II, Marian's followers looked to that prophecy. Her spirits had been right in their prophecy!

However, was World War II the worst war the world will ever see? Could that prophecy have been speaking of another island and an even greater, more horrific war? A war that has not yet come.

Anyone that met her would attest to the fact that she was honest in her belief and that her character was beyond reproach. People would tell stories of things she said, facts she quoted that were unknown to her. These people claimed she was able to do this so often as to limit the likelihood of it being merely chance.

But were they right or just followers that refused to see outside of their belief? Certainly there was doubt and skepticism in the minds of psychologists and critics but not in the mind of Marian. They created the exotic nature of the work and they knew the true meaning of the symbolic images she painted. They directed her hand to foretell what was to come. She couldn't give a date when the foretelling would occur because there was no time where they existed. They saw with unlimited vision – without dates or times. They only knew it would happen.

On February 24, 1946, Marian Spore Bush left this world. Were her mother and sister there for her when her ship of death arrived? Did she finally get to meet the spirits who guided her in life? What a glorious reunion that must have been.

Marian completed hundreds of paintings over her lifetime. Possibly more. No one kept track. Sadly, most of her work has vanished. Only a handful of paintings remain.

As I scanned over the images in the book she wrote called *They*, I was fascinated by the work revealed within the pages. Much of the symbolic imagery was beyond explanation.

"World Aflame", one of Marian's last spirit paintings. What does it foretell - global warming, a meteor striking the world, or a major nuclear war? (Marian S. Bush)

There was one painting that I found especially interesting. She completed it around 1939. The title was World on Fire. It showed the world as a circular ball of pure black. No features were seen on the globe. No land. No water. Only blackness.

In the painting was a massive demon-like face blowing at the darkened world, flames bursting from the demon's mouth, swirling around the earth, heating it, burning it. No one, including Marian, had any idea of its meaning.

It may have represented many things. However, my mind was immediately drawn to two possibilities. A representation of global warming or a global war leading to a nuclear holocaust of monumental proportions.

There is another painting, created in 1938. It showed an angry-looking man with dark skin and a large, aquiline nose. He wore a keffiyeh (turban/headdress). His face dominated the painting as he looked over a valley of crucified men.

Marian called the painting "Crucifixion of the Jew." It was completed in 1938, not long before the onset of World War II.

In 1938, Hitler's insane desire to destroy the Jews was well known. His horrific concentration camps had been holding Jews since 1933. At the time, people considered Crucifixion of the Jew a painting of the time and not prophetic.

However, if the painting was symbolic of Hitler's insane attempt to destroy the Jewish race, why was the threatening face overlooking the valley of death a dark-skinned man wearing a Keffiyeh and not the face of Hitler or, at the least, a light-skinned face?

There was a painting I desperately wanted to find. One of Marian's last. The painting was not in Marian's book. I was unable to find it in the remaining archives of her work. I even attempted to contact descendants of the Spores and Bushes without luck.

The painting was described in various 1946 newspapers. There are two airplanes headed towards a cityscape. Sky-rise buildings fill the canvas with prominent tall towers. Black clouds of smoke and flame cover the sky. She titled the painting, "New York City: When?"

**"But this I know—beyond this strife
There is no pain.
Somewhere the flowers bloom again
Death is not death—it's life."**

~ Irving T. Bush.

Direct Voice Medium

The year was 1847. It was a time of innocence. A time when people were more trusting, open and vulnerable to the whims and trickery of others. Adding to that was a growing curiosity, a rising desire to know what happens after the physical body dies. People prayed that their deceased loved ones would somehow find a way to send them a final word of hope from the other side.

Indeed, it was a time of great spiritual need that would lead the way to one of America's most powerful, mysterious movements – Spiritualism. Spiritualism is the belief that those in the afterlife have the ability and interest to communicate with the living and are able to do so through special, gifted people called mediums.

The world was ready. The birth of Spiritualism began.

It was in1847, John and Margaret Fox, along with their two youngest daughters, Kate and Margaretta (Maggie), moved to the small community of Hydesville, New York. After a short while, the family began hearing strange bumps, knocks and bangs that made them believe the home was haunted.

One evening, Kate and Maggie thought they might be able to communicate with the spirits residing in the home and

Photo opposite: A seance in the 1920s. (public domain)

began asking questions. To the surprise and awe of their parents, the girls received knocks in response.

After several similar family gatherings, the parents were convinced their daughters had a special gift of spirit communication. Soon many others believed. By 1849 the girls were doing public gatherings.

Their sister Leah soon joined them to help keep things organized. It wasn't long after that the popularity of the Fox sisters grew to momentous proportions. With them came the birth of Modern Spiritualism. The girls traveled the world demonstrating their incredible ability to communicate with the spirits.

Many skeptics routinely exposed their methods of trickery. In spite of that, the spiritualist movement continued to expand. New, more creative mediums gained popularity and interest in the Fox sisters declined. By the late 1880's they had developed a drinking problem and money was becoming a real issue.

In 1888, a reporter offered the women $1500 to confess that it was all trickery. Kate and Maggie stepped up to that offer that some called a bribe and did something unthinkable. They publicly confessed it had all been faked. They did not have special powers.

The Fox sisters began the spiritualist movement. L to R: Kate, Leah, and Margaret (public domain)

Their devoted followers were horrified. The sisters attempted to recant that confession but it was too late. A few years later, both Kate and Maggie died in poverty.

Many believed their confession was driven by the need for money. Even the skeptical Harry Houdini believed it. Were the ladies gifted or fake? Whatever the case, they died broken and destitute. Their confession, however, didn't slow down the growth of the spiritualism movement.

In the ashes of the Fox sisters came a new form of spirit communication. It was the physical medium. A physical medium was capable of making spirits materialize in various ways. A materialist could bring forth a visual apparition, and a direct voice medium could bring forth the actual voice of the spirit.

Most physical mediums performed in total darkness. They would sit behind curtains or in small, enclosed rooms or a closet, referred to as a Spirit Cabinet. According to the medium, the purpose of this was to give them the ability to achieve higher levels of consciousness.

During the séance, a substance referred to as ectoplasm would emerge. This would be expelled through the medium's mouth, ears or nose. It was said that spirits would take this

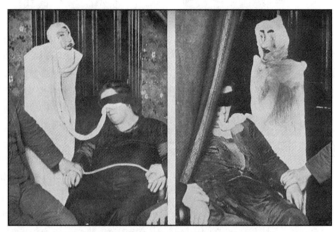

Use of the Spirit Cabinet was common among mediums. The cabinet was like a magician's magic box of tricks. Here, fake ectoplasm is revealed. (public domain)

substance and use it to be seen or heard in our world.

According to spiritualist belief, ectoplasm was very light sensitive and, if exposed to light, would retreat into the physical medium's body, causing serious physical injury or even death.

A tool of the physical mediums was the spirit trumpet. This was used to amplify spirit audio responses. A spiritualist trumpet was a relatively slender conical device standing about three feet tall and approximately 7 inches in diameter. It came in multiple sections that would collapse one into the other, allowing for easy storage and transport. This instrument would sometimes levitate, moving from person to person and halting near the individual the spirit wished to communicate with.

Of course, the way mediums worked left them open to ridicule by the skeptics who firmly believed it was all trickery. It would be easy to deceive people in darkness.

Etta Wreidt, Direct Voice Medium
(public domain)

Indeed, the Spirit Cabinet was the medium's magic box. String, wire or other devices could be hidden away for them or their assistants to simulate spirit activity. Very thin gauze could be hidden in their box to simulate a spirit or ectoplasm. Some mediums even swallowed the gauze and regurgitated it during the séance. The audible sound of a spirit voice was merely the medium using ventriloquism.

Other tricks that were used were a toe wedged under a table leg for table tipping. A slender rod, unseen in the darkness, could be used to move the trumpet from person to person. There were, in fact, all manner of methods used for deception.

Greater numbers of people came forward claiming to be mediums and with these increasing numbers came individuals whose goal was to reveal their fraud. Skeptics referred to mediums as the Great Magicians, preying on desperate people.

In 1882, the United Kingdom formed the Society for Psychical Research (SPR). Just two years later the American Society for Psychical Research (ASPR) began. Members of these groups were highly respected, well-educated scientists, chemists, doctors and lay people. Their purpose was to scientifically and objectively evaluate each medium for possible fakery. Through their efforts the work of mediums, one after the other after the other, was debunked as their deceitful tricks were revealed.

Then came Etta Wriedt. Her life was a mystery. There are very few photographs of Etta Wriedt. She didn't like photographs and she didn't talk about her past.

She once said, "I have never had my photo taken since I was a little girl; and as to my life being printed, I don't really care for it. Let people remember me as they knew me. My life is of no interest to investigators. My work speaks for itself."[1]

Etta was born Henrietta Knapp on December 10, 1861 (some historical records state 1862) in a small New York town called Oswego. As far as schooling, Etta didn't make it past the 8th grade. Of course, that was not uncommon in those days. She could read, write and add numbers. That was enough.

Standing just 5' 5" with a slender build, light brown hair and blue eyes, she was unimposing. Her voice was quiet, gentle, and refined. Nothing in her appearance or manner was flamboyant, nothing in her demeanor that would suggest the fame and recognition she would one day have.

As a teenager through her early 20's, Etta made a living cleaning the homes of others, serving in the capacity as domestic housekeeper. In 1886, while living in Dayton, Ohio, she met the man who would be her husband, Phillip Wriedt. They married in 1889. Though childless, the couple remained very close throughout their years together.

It was in the 1890's that her practice as a direct-voice medium began to skyrocket. In April 1898, Etta was asked to perform a seance in Toronto. In attendance was the well-known Canadian journalist, Phillips Thompson. That session lasted three hours. Phillips would later describe this experience as wonderous.[2]

Admiral W. Usborne Moore, a retired and respected British naval commander, heard of this new American direct-voice medium at his home in England. He wanted to meet her.

---

1 King, John Sumptner, *Dawn of the Awakened Mind* (New York: The James McCann Company, 1920), 80.
2 Levine, Allen, *King: Lyone Mackenzie King, a Life Guided by the Hand of Destiny* (Douglas and McIntyre, 2013), 250-251.

The Admiral prided himself on logical thinking and his ability to weigh the facts of each situation with a high degree of objectivity. He had once been a strong agnostic and openly denounced the teachings of the church. Moore did not hold back his expression of doubt at any form of afterlife.

Admiral W. Usborne Moore, respected member of the SPR and a supporter of Etta Wreidt (public domain)

That belief would be challenged when he became curious about the spiritualist movement. He joined the SPR and suddenly found himself immersed in the world of spiritualism. It was then, he had said, his eyes were opened to the reality of the afterlife. He became a believer.

The Admiral came to Detroit, Michigan specifically to meet Etta Wriedt, who was living with her husband in a small, understated home on Bailey Street. Moore attended several séances. Weeks later, he returned to England, stunned by what he had experienced. He praised her skills, claiming she was the most remarkable direct voice medium he had ever witnessed.

In 1911, W. T. Stead, a well-known British journalist and high-ranking member of the SPR, invited her to his home in Kensington. So it was that Etta Wriedt, now in her early 50's, a former housekeeper with an 8th grade education, began a journey that would make her an international star and leader in spiritualism.

People said Etta was different than other mediums. She didn't work with an assistant or have anyone help her during a séance. She did not confine herself to a Spirit Closet. She would not sit behind a curtain, or other enclosures commonly used in trickery. Nor did she go into a trance. Instead, she would sit with her guests around any table and remain fully alert throughout the séance.

In a book written by Admiral Moore in 1912 called *The Voices*, he recounted dozens and dozens of séances conducted by Etta while she was in England. At first, the séances described weren't that different from other mediums. Rooms were completely darkened. Spirit lights appeared and would float and move about in the air above and around Etta. There were many ways to fake this for the skilled medium.

Although she was a direct voice medium and not a materialist (i.e., a spiritualist who brings forward the physical form of the spirit), she would sometimes produce the physical image. When someone would say the image did not look like their loved one, Etta would explain that's because it is an ethereal image, which often makes the spirit appear different than when they were in physical body.

Of course, the skeptic would laugh at such a notion. However, to the believers that explanation made complete sense.

Etta had a spirit guide as many medium did. This was a spirit attached to her that opened the portal to the spirit world. His name was Dr. John Sharp. He claimed to have been born in Glasgow during the 18th Century but was taken to American when he was very young, eventually dying in Evansville, Indiana.

No research was completed by the SPR to determine whether there had ever been a Dr. Sharp. Records dating to the 18th century, of course, are very scarce and validating his existence may not have been a critical part of the group's assessment of her mediumship.

Etta often used a spirit trumpet. This was a typical tool for spirit communication. It would emit popping sounds and fly up (levitate) sometimes hitting a sitter (the term used to describe guests attending the séance). Voices would come through the trumpet. Some so quiet the other sitters could not hear. Yet, other times, the voices were strong, clear and heard by all.

William Thomas Stead, well-known English newspaper editor and author. A key member of the Society for Psychical Research. He foresaw his death on the Titanic. (public domain)

Based on the first series of described séances, there was nothing unusual in her methods and some were almost laughable in their absurdity. However, as the journal entries continued, things became more interesting.

Not all séances were conducted in complete darkness. In fact, on a number of occasions they were done in someone's home, in full daylight or in a room lit by gas or electric lights. Although in full light, the spirit visions were not seen but the voices were heard. There is no question it was the voices Etta brought forward that distinguished her from the other mediums.

According to guests, communications from loved ones were absolutely accurate. Although apparently the spirit's ethereal image may not resemble the physical body, the voices heard were much as they were in life.

Sitters would remark how the sound of the voice, the accent, intonations and type of words used or special nicknames applied were exactly the way their loved ones had sounded. The spirit would often share little known things, secrets that only the sitter and their deceased loved one knew.

One example is the story of a woman who had lost her son. In life, they had always shared a little joke. She had told him he should never leave the house without some gold in his pocket and had given him a small gold nugget. He had always carried that nugget with him.

The day of his burial, before the casket was closed, she had slipped the small gold nugget under her son's shirt. Even her husband had not known she had done that. Yet, when the spirit of her son came through, he thanked her and told her he'd found the nugget where she had placed it. He told her he would keep it with him even though things like that were not needed where he was.

Another time, the spirit of a deceased wife came forward. She and her husband talked at great length about things so personal Moore decided not to include what was said in his book. At some point, the spirit of his wife mentioned that she wanted him to keep certain pieces of her jewelry and not give it all away to family, which was something he had apparently been doing. She described, in great detail, which pieces she wanted him to keep. These were things he had given to her and were of special meaning to them both.

There is even an account in the book *Mysteries and Secrets: The 16-Book Complete Codex: Dex/Mysteries* where a duchess invited Etta to Warwick Castle because of the amount of paranormal experiences encountered there. Etta's things were brought to her room ahead of her arrival. The Duchess saw one of Etta's trumpets and couldn't resist. She put it to her ear and was shocked to hear the voice of her husband, King Edward VII, speak to her. She said they carried on a complete conversation in German. The King came back to her at several sessions with Etta in the Castle.

A séance would last from 45 minutes to several hours. During that time, Etta might bring forth up to 14 or 15 spirits. Not all voices came through the trumpet. Many were heard in the very air surrounding the sitters. Conversations between the spirit and their loved one might be just a few seconds, other times they would be full conversations over an extended time.

The skeptic, of course, would say she must have done her research to gather such personal information on these people. That would be a likely possibility except for the fact that she did not always know in advance who was coming or, if she did, might only know a day or two ahead of the séance. Add to that the fact she had as many as 18 people at a time. To bring 14

Arthur Conan Doyle, author of the Sherlock Holmes book series and a founder of the Society for Psychical Research. (public domain)

or 15 spirits forward during one sitting, each sharing very personal stories while using the right tone and accent of the deceased person would require a good deal of preparation and an excellent memory and seems too complex to even consider likely.

Another fascinating aspect of her sessions was that there were often international guests in attendance. When the spirit who came through was attached to someone from a foreign country, they would converse in their native language. According to Admiral Moore, languages spoken included Croatian, French, Belgium, German, Swiss, Italian, Romanian, Serbian and others. Her sitters swore the voices were true and accents perfect.

Perhaps even more compelling, there sometimes were several spirit conversations going on at the same time. During those conversations, it was not unusual for Etta to be speaking to someone else at the table or conversing freely with one of the spirits. It was said the conversations were as natural as you would speak to them in life.

Of course, not every session brought forth spirits. Unproductive sessions were called blank séances. Sometimes a month would pass without result. Etta could give no reason for these blank séances other than the atmosphere may be wrong, she was too tired or perhaps the spirits and sitters weren't receptive. Her followers believed her blank séances were a confirmation of her honesty. If she were a fake, every séance would be productive.

There were times Etta became melancholy. She wondered why she could bring forth the spirit of loved ones for others but not for herself. She wanted very much to speak with members of her family but they never came through. Never. This is another part of Etta's mystery. She didn't speak of her family or her past and yet she mourned for them. Why she wouldn't speak of them remains unknown to this day.

Many esteemed members of the SPR observed her performances. This included Sir William Barrett, a noted physicist and co-founder of the organization; Sir Oliver Lodge, known for his advancements in electricity and radio; Sir Arthur Conan Doyle, the physician who created the Sherlock Holmes book series; Dr. John S. King, founder of the Canadian branch of the SPR; and, of course, Admiral W. Usborne Moore.

They closely evaluated her methods, attempting to identify possible use of tricks. They were, however, left without reasonable explanation other than she was actually communicating with the dead. Sir Arthur Conan Doyle, along with members of the SPR, proclaimed her to be the World's Best Direct Voice Medium.

The critics wondered if the SPR was objectively evaluating her abilities using appropriate testing methods or were they overlooking obvious trickery to strengthen their cause? There was growing criticism of the SPR. Skeptics said the group had ulterior motives in their assessment of spiritualists. Although the SPR had revealed many fraudulent mediums, it wasn't enough. The critics believed the SPR was really formed to cling to something spiritual and used their organization to validate mediums even when their validation methods were biased or incomplete.

Of course, there were other investigators, people who came to evaluate her performance. She would willingly sit wherever they wanted her to sit, in whatever light conditions they preferred, anything they wanted to help rule out fraud. They, too, tested her and could find no trickery.

Etta Wreidt's popularity grew. She found herself traveling to England, Scotland, Norway, and other European cities with all expenses paid. Although she only charged $1.00 per person (a nominal fee), she did accept donations or gifts when attendees were especially pleased with the results of their sessions. Because she often held séances for the elite, it seems likely her donations were substantial.

It was April 10, 1912. W. T. Stead was leaving Southampton headed to America. When he returned in May, he planned on bringing Etta Wriedt with him.

Etta looked forward to spending time in England. She enjoyed the county and the people. This time, however, she was unsettled. Something wasn't right.

W. T. Stead also appeared unusually somber in the days leading up to his trip to America. He told his assistant, Edith Harper, that something was going to happen, somewhere, or somehow. And that it will be "for good."[3] He had a strong sense of doom. He even gave Edith instructions regarding his business affairs should he not return.

The Titanic left that evening at 7:00 p.m. with W. T. Stead on it. Five days later it would go down and Stead would never be seen again.

---

3 Tymyn, Michael. "Remembering Titanic Victim William T. Stead 100 Years Later | Michael Tymn Blog on White Crow Books." White Crow Books, 2 Apr. 2012, whitecrowbooks.com/michaeltymn/entry/remembering_titanic_victim_william_t._stead_100_years_later.

Several survivors of that dreadful time remembered seeing Stead on board. Although he was clearly frightened, he remained outwardly stoic, in control. At one point he was seen sitting, reading a book. Another time, calmly helping people into lifeboats. He was last seen standing near the helm watching as the last lifeboat drifted away.

Etta was in New York when the disaster happened. Reports suggest she immediately knew something was wrong. Even before word got back that the Titanic was lost at sea, she knew Stead was gone.

Three days after his passing, his spirit voice came through during one of her séances. At first the voice was quite weak, although clear enough to be understood. The first communication was very brief. The next day it was stronger and the following day stronger yet. Major-General Alfred Turner, in attendance at Etta's séance, knew Stead very well and said the voice was unmistakably him.

Stead spoke of the events that transpired prior to the sinking and gave considerable detail about his death. He recalled a sharp blow to the head and a brief struggle to take a breath before waking into a new existence.

He said he saw hundreds of spirits around him, souls who did not yet know their physical bodies were gone. They were fighting the transition, grouping around in the dark begging for light. He said he was helping them understand and become enlightened to their new existence and that the new existence was glorious.

He encouraged Etta to continue with the plan to go to England. Although she still had a sense of foreboding, she decided to keep the planned trip and arrived in Southampton in early May. There was indeed trouble afoot for this venerable direct-voice medium.

At the beginning of that same year, 1912, a brilliant although eccentric Norwegian scientist, Kristian Birkeland, was going through a divorce. Obsession with his research in atmospheric electric currents gave him little free time for other things in his life including his wife, Ida. Now she was leaving him. He was devastated and angry. He had given her every-thing. How could she do this to him?

Adding to his stress was the work he was doing on atmospheric currents. His credible theories and thorough research were being disputed, dismissed and ridiculed by his peers. He felt disrespected. He had been nominated for the Nobel Prize seven times! How dare they denigrate and challenge his knowledge and his work? Birkeland was angry and becoming a bit neurotic with the first stage of paranoia taking over. He sometimes thought people were out to get him. He was taking medication to sleep but even that sometimes didn't work.

On that cold winter's morning in 1912, he was just trying to get through the process of divorce as quickly and painlessly as possible. That's what brought him to the office of his attorney, Johan Bredal. After signing divorce papers, the two men went to lunch. That's when Bredal asked for the scientist's help.

Bredal has been elected to an organization called the Norwegian Society For Psychic Research (NSPR) at the encouragement of friends. They wanted him to attend a séance of the famous medium, Etta Wriedt. This Mrs. Wriedt had been to Norway before and caused quite a stir. Her talents were claimed to be truly remarkable. The committee was being organized to observe, scrutinize and challenge her abilities. He wanted Birkeland to head the committee.

Bredal went on to share his disdain for spiritualism, believing it was nothing but trickery and that its very nature was driving humanity back to the Dark Ages. Birkeland agreed and was happy to lead the committee. In fact, he was looking forward to exposing the lies and ignorance of this American medium.

Kristian Birkeland, the scientist who claimed to have identified Etta as a fraud. (public domain)

The seances with Etta Wriedt began on August 12, 1912 in Christiania (now Oslo), Norway. Birkeland was joined by three others, one of whom was an editor and journalist. Three séances were attended.

During those sessions the spirit trumpet was used. At one session, Birkeland briefly examined the device and was about to blow into it but was stopped by Etta. She claimed blowing into the trumpet would prevent the spirits from responding through it.

Birkeland looked at her skeptically, shrugged, sat back and quietly observed. During the sessions, the trumpet made noises and moved. On a few occasions it jumped as much as three feet, hitting one of the sitters.

When the session concluded, the lights were turned on and Birkeland quickly went to the trumpet, picked it up, smelled the inside and smiled. He got her!

Birkeland prepared a report exposing Etta Wriedt as a fraud. An article appeared in the August 25, 1912 edition of Aftenposten, one of Norway's largest newspapers.

He explained how he had discovered her trickery. Upon picking up the trumpet he immediately noticed moisture inside which had not been there earlier. Next he reported the smell of a chemical gas that he claimed was potassium. It would explode if exposed to moisture. It was a scathing article. He went so far as to call her a monster and a cunning swindler.

Needless to say, his comment created tremendous controversy. Those who knew and had experienced séances with Etta were outraged. There was no proof of what he said. No testing was done to validate his claim. Only his word. What scientist makes a statement as fact without proper testing? He was clearly biased and obsessed by his need to disclaim spiritualists.

Besides, the trumpet was only a very small part of Etta's séances. What about the voices … the visions? Could he explain that? He didn't bother to respond. It wasn't needed in his mind. Use of one piece of trickery, to him, debunked everything else. A lie in one is a lie in all. And he was far too busy to bother with her again.

Etta was devastated and retreated to her close circle of friends in England where she continued to conduct seances. W. T. Stead came through several more times.

He was seen both visually and in spirit voice. His closest friends, secretary and daughter saw his image manifest from the darkness. They claimed it was his exact likeness. He bowed to them, greeting each personally and shared antidotes from their past. His movements were fluid, smooth. It was said he looked and sounded much like he had in life. He was happy. There was no fear. It was a joyful existence.

Etta Wriedt eventually returned to her home on Baldwin Street in Detroit and to her dear husband, Phillip. Although her rising star had been tarnished by Birkeland's harsh words, it didn't stop her work. She returned to England and Europe several times.

Sadly, she lost Phillip on December 11, 1925, one day after her 64th birthday. Whether she was ever able to communicate with him in death is unknown. Etta passed on September 14, 1942 at her home on Baldwin Street in Detroit. She never returned.

This story isn't quite over. We need to share a bit more on Kristian Birkeland, the brilliant scientist who was the only man to call Etta a fraud.

As mentioned earlier, Birkeland had been obsessing over his research and findings on atmospheric electric current. He was more and more upset that his peers dismissed what he had so obviously proven to be true.

One day he would be vindicated. His theories and research were absolutely accurate and his theories would be used to explain the phenomena known as Aurora Borealis and much more. Unfortunately, this didn't happen until decades after his death.

Perhaps even more interesting is his controversial conclusion regarding Etta Wriedt's trickery. Even if there was a potassium/water mixture inside the trumpet, he never was able to explain how she managed to generate multiple, simultaneous spirit voice communications or have those voices speak fluently in at least 12 languages.

It would also be discovered, after his exposing report on Etta, that Birkeland's wife, Ida, had been consulting with Etta Wriedt for some time. She had kept their sessons secret from her husband.

Birkeland had been shocked and very upset upon learning this. He swore he had found out after his decision on Etta and that it was not a factor in his decison. However, is that completely true? Certainly if he had discovered that prior to his attending Etta's séance, it would have created a motive to discredit her, a possible reason for his report to be so scathing, dismissive and venomous enough to call Etta a monster.

After the infamous August 1912 sessions with Etta, Birkeland's paranoia grew. The paranoia stemmed from something he had invented. It was a device to be used for war. He submitted it to the French government, who, after testing, declined the proposal. Birkeland then went to the British government, who also declined it.

From that point on, Birkeland believed British spies were following him. He worried constantly, even buying a gun, which he kept on his bedside table. The scientist began having problem sleeping and started taking a drug called Veronal to help calm him down. The paranoia grew. Birkeland's health declined.

In June 1917, he went to visit some colleagues in Tokyo, Japan. During that time, he rarely left his room, calling servants to bring him more writing paper or coffee but no food. He remained this way for at least two weeks – not eating or sleeping, completely obsessed with writing his ground-breaking paper.

Finally, June 13, 1917, although physically weak, he left the hotel. From there he made it to the telegraph office and sent a message to his attorney and friend, Johan Bredal.

Two days later, June 15, there was no response from his room and an employee of the hotel entered. Birkelan's body was found lying on the bed.

A loaded pistol sat on his bedside table. It would be discovered he had taken10g of his sleeping medication instead of the prescribed 0.5g. Most people considered his death a suicide. The reason was unknown.

Birkeland's paper, the last of his work, sat on the table in his room. The document was something so important he spent the last days of his life completing it. The paper was carefully packaged and sent on a ship to England.

As fate would have it, the ship carrying this important paper went down in a violent storm at sea. The ship and all crew disappeared. Birkeland's ground-breaking paper was lost. What was his last study? What did it involve? It will always remain an unknown.

Meanwhile, back in England, Johan Bredal sat in his office staring down at Kristian Birkeland's telegram, the one he had sent off shortly before his death. Bredan was perplexed. What had Birkeland been trying to tell him? The telegram contained just three words: Remember Wriedt Committee.

Finally, Bredal believed he knew the meaning. Birkeland wanted him to hold a séance and he wanted Etta Wriedt to do it. If there was any way to come through, he would. Incredible.

It is unknown if Bredal and the committee asked Etta to hold a séance. She was at her home in Detroit when Birkeland died. Passport and ship records suggest Etta didn't return to England and Europe for several years after his death. There are no records to suggest she was involved in any of the séances to contact Birkeland. However, several séances were held; the paranoid albeit brilliant scientist never came through.

In the world of spiritualism, Etta Wriedt remains one of the most well-known, respected direct-voice mediums of her time. Was she a fake? Was she a Great Magician or the Greatest Direct-Voice Medium of All Time? That is for this reader to decide.

No Way Out for the Killing Witch

Twelve of Her Boarders Died Before She Went to Prison, Another Afterward—And Now She's In for Life.

The Way the Jury Figured, William Veres Was as Guilty as His Mother.

By GERALD DUNCAN

FREEDOM'S door has been slammed on the Witch of Delray. The air she breathes for the rest of her days must be screened through prison bars. There will be no recapture of the years when she roamed the streets of Detroit and killing men.

The Witch of Delray, who actually is Mrs. Rose Veres, murdered for profit, which is why she was sentenced to life imprisonment in Michigan in 1931. For a time, while lawyers were fighting desperately for a new trial for her, it looked as though she might be free again. But now Recorder's Judge John J. Maher, at Detroit, has denied her appeal.

Mrs. Veres made a good thing of being a witch. She got away with it for seven years, during which time she became a legendary figure in black, and by the time the law caught up with her the number of her victims was reckoned at 12. Her bank deposits for the period totaled $68,000.

She worked out a simple plan for living by the death of others. She took a rooming house in the Delray section of Detroit, where most of her lodgers were—like herself—Hungarian-born. They were simple folk and Mrs. Veres volunteered to look after their money. At the same time she insured their lives.

When police got interested in the goings-on in her home they uncovered 75 insurance policies on her boarders, in all of which she was the beneficiary. She had a reason why.

"I kept insurance policies on most of my boarders," she said, "because that is the way my people do. We want a good funeral. There must be flowers and lodge members. I gave everyone a fine funeral."

The police thought too many fine funerals were being held at the frame dwelling on Medina Street.

They became curious when Steven Mak, 68, tumbled from a ladder outside the Veres household and died of a fractured skull. They began asking questions and soon discovered he was the twelfth man to die at the Medina St. house since Sept. 21, 1924, when Steven Sebastian suffered what was described on the death certificate as a fatal cerebral hemorrhage.

After a little inquiring in the neighborhood they found Marie Chevalla, 11, who was making mud-pies outside her home when Mak fell.

"I saw Mr. Mak go up the ladder," she said. "Mrs. Veres was holding it for him at the attic window. He was right at the attic window. He swayed and moaned as if he was sick."

Her story spun a web around the Witch of Delray when she added:

"While he was falling, Mrs. Veres and William (her son) poked their heads out of the window."

Yes, that was right, Mrs. Veres remembered. She had asked Mak to repair a window. But the police said the window didn't need repairs.

Then there was the story of John Walker. Mrs. Veres, he said, told him to water the ground where the ladder rested and the Witch herself placed it on the slippery clay. And there was $4,180 insurance on Mak's life.

A jury believed that Mrs. Veres and her son pushed Mak to death

Steven Mak, Fixing a Window, Swayed, Fell, Died. An Accident, Surely—Until a Child Told What She Had Seen.

Mrs. Rose Veres Murdere—For Profit—While She ing Known as the Witch

and returned a verdict th the maximum penalty u gan law for both—life im

Responsibility for th deaths wasn't proved a Veres. But the police many strange circumstan delved into her dusty pas

They learned that he Gabor, and Laszlo Toth, were working on a car i garage one day in 1927 deny the door slammed of carbon monoxide poi erated by the automobile

They heard about names were known as J Balit Peterman, es, Steven Faist rio, Berni Kalo ivon and John C of them slept o cots in the dirt lar. All of ther of wine betwee All of them died their deaths wer lye in the wine.

While all these thing pening, Mrs. Veres wa known around the neight sinister character.

Some said she was bor set of teeth and a veil, said:

"If she wants, she herself into a wolf or a b

That's how she becam of Delray and why she w both adults and children.

Although prison clai spell continues.

Almost two years af jailed John Kampfl, one ment lodgers, cut his thr not a critical wound. Do would recover.

"No," he said. "The her evil eye on me."

The next morning he probably isn't the reason refused her a new trial. But who knows?

House of Funerals

From the beginning of human life, reverence was given to the powers that created sun, earth, wind, fire and water. As civilization evolved, the powers that controlled these elements became gods. To honor and respect these gods, they developed rituals and from that grew religion.

With religion came superstitions and the belief that some of the living possessed great supernatural powers They were called werewolves, shape shifters, vampires, and witches. Their existence, to that earlier civilization, was unquestionable and as real as the earth on which we live.

Witchcraft, many scholars believe, predates most religions known today, going back to the Paleolithic period 40,000 years ago. Wicca or Wicce comes from Old English and its interpreted as meaning "wise one." What they practiced was Witchcraft (craft of the wise).

It was believed that witches could foretell the future and were capable of doing both good and evil. As Christianity evolved, witchcraft was considered heresy and those involved were evil and wicked. Common folk thought a witch had given his or her soul to Satan and from that received malevolent, supernatural powers to harm others.

Photo opposite: Full-page article appearing in The American Weekly, Feb. 18, 1945. (Hearst Publications)

Europe was the heart of the witch frenzy. In the 1600's, it migrated to America ending in the infamous witchcraft trials of Salem, Massachusetts. Twenty people were executed for witchcraft in Salem with five others dying in jail.

Europe was far worse. By the time the witch-hunt hysteria ended in the late 1700's, the estimated number of those executed range from 30,000 to over 60,000. The majority of these people were women.

Why women? It was thought women were targeted because of the enduring fear that they were able to control men and thereby coerce, for their own purposes, a male-dominated Christian society into corruption and eternal damnation. Similar to the Biblical story of what Eve did to Adam.

Just because the primary witch-hunt obsession ended doesn't mean fear of witches and their evil practices did. In the 19th and 20th centuries many still whispered behind closed doors that a witch's curse was the cause when crops failed or chickens stopped producing eggs or sudden illness and death swept a village.

Even today there are those who believe and fear the power of witchcraft. Is there any basis for that fear? I have interviewed a number of Wiccans (the modern term for those practicing witchcraft) and they tell me no.

Wiccans don't give their souls to the devil. In fact, they don't even believe in the devil. They also don't believe in one God. They have faith in many gods and goddesses; witchcraft affirms the divinity in all things, including cycles in nature and lunar phases. Their faith focuses on the powers of nature and the environment to create positive change.

A Wiccan's philosophy is "do no harm." Doing evil or dark spells is not part of their creed. Their reason is karma and their belief in three-fold. What you do to others will come back to you three times worse. For this reason, they stay away from doing anything negative to anyone.

Do all Wiccans follow this creed? One Wiccan I spoke with said, "It's a little like Christianity. You're not supposed to use the Lord's name in vain. Yet, many do."

One man I spoke with was a Warlock (male witch) and called himself Jacob. Jacob did acknowledge he had used, on rare occasions, what some refer to as black magic which is a spell with a negative effect.

What he said was this. "Bad or good is somewhat subjective. What is bad for one person may be good for another. There are selfish people with intent to harm others everywhere in the world. Would a spell cast to stop that person from harming be bad?"

I asked if that might mean ending someone's life?

"You can prevent someone from doing harm without their death being involved," he responded.

My next question was direct. "Would you have the power to cause another's death? Are you capable of casting a spell on someone you don't really know—a spell that would cause heart failure or serious illness?"

There was a long pause before his quiet yet confident response, "Yes."

Yes. His answer stayed with me for quite some time. Was he being truthful or just spinning a story for my benefit? My logical mind tells me it's just a story. Yet I wonder what untapped power does the mind have to control others?

Rose Veres never questioned her ability to do exactly that—control the fate of others. She had great power, or so she claimed. She was Michigan's most infamous witch and was known as the Witch of Delray.

Rose was born in Hungary and immigrated to America around 1911. Not long after her arrival in America, she married Joseph Sebestyn, a Russian immigrant. They had one child, William, born in 1914. Unfortunately, Rose and Joseph's marriage was short lived. He died the same year his son was born, December 1914, from "cancer of the face."

Not long after Joseph's death, Rose met and married a second time. He was a man six years her junior named Gabor Veres. Gabor worked as a laborer in the Detroit salt mines.[1]

---

1 The tunnels of these salt mines still exist under the city of Detroit to this day.

The couple owned a small home at 7894 Medina Street in the Hungarian settlement of Delray located near the Detroit River, south of Fort Street near Jefferson Avenue. At the time it was considered a suburb of Detroit. Medina was a narrow street just a block long that was lined with small

Detroit, 1917, a time of high employment and rapidly forming immigrant communities. (public domain)

frame homes. It was skirted on one side by a railroad. The other side was blocked from traffic and served as a playground for the children.

Immigrant settlements were very cloistered in those earlier days and their communities self-contained with stores, churches, and gathering places. There was no need to leave except for work. Delray was such a community. Its Hungarian residents stayed tightly within its borders.

Medina Street, in fact, was a world unto itself. The City of Detroit and its big city turmoil were far from the Hungarian people who lived there. Most of the residents and boarders on Medina came from a particular area of Hungary called Magyrs.

This area of Hungary is steeped in supernatural belief. Witches were common in Magyrs, not just witches but also vampires, evil spirits, wolfmen and wolf-women. The people of Magyrs claimed to have heard the horrible cries of these supernatural beings when someone in their village died.

It didn't matter that they no longer lived in Hungry. Witches, vampires, and wolfmen still existed. It was a fact. Other people could believe what they wanted but the Hungarian people knew the truth. There was little question in their minds that Rose Veres was exactly who she professed to be, a witch of great power.

Like others on Medina Street had done, Gabor and Rose decided to board tenants at their home to make a little extra income and ran a dosshouse or, as it was sometimes called, a flophouse. A flophouse was cheap lodging for low income people. Medina Street had several operating dosshouses.

The Veres' tenants there were all Hungarian men each speaking little, if any, English. Freshly immigrated, they had no family in America and limited income. These men were not used to luxury and the Veres' dosshouse was affordable; it kept a roof over their heads.

Things were going along rather well. Rose and Gabor had their first child around 1916, and named him Gabor Jr. Then came Elizabeth. Tragically, the little girl would live only one month, dying from inanition in 1917. Inanition is extreme malnutrition, death resulting from lack of food and water. Their last child was named John.

Records suggest there was a change in Rose after the death of her daughter, Elizabeth. She became quieter, more introverted. Had her baby girl's death been the result of their neglect or more the fact that Rose's milk wasn't sufficient to sustain the little babe? Did Rose feel guilt? Whatever the situation, her personality changed.

The first death in the Veres' dosshouse occurred around 1923. The boarder's cause of death was alcoholism. Sometime later, another boarder died; the cause was also alcoholism. Rose had life insurance policies for both men and quickly cashed them. With part of that money, she gave them very good funerals. In those days that meant a good casket, flowers at the funeral home, and a burial plot at a local cemetery.

Then, in February 1924, another misfortune hit the Veres home. Gabor and one of their boarders, Louis Toth, died from asphyxiation. Apparently, the two men were working on a car when the garage door, unknown to them, tightly closed. They were later found dead, lying under the car. Fortunately for Rose, she had insurance policies for both her husband and Louis. Again, she gave both men wonderful funerals, which still left enough insurance money to help get her through the grief.

So began the series of deaths at the Veres' boarding home. Most, according to death records, were from natural causes including alcohol poisoning, intestinal problems, or organ failure. Of course, one boarder did hang himself in the basement of the home. Obviously that wasn't from natural causes. It was thought, however, that the man was very depressed, a sad problem that many poor immigrants faced in their new country. Three more died mysteriously with their cause of death undetermined.

Rose's tenants grew nervous and a bit fearful that Rose was giving the evil eye to her boarders, causing their deaths. At least one left in fear. His name was John Kempfl, and he claimed Rose had given him the evil eye. We'll share more about John's mysterious death later in the story.

One glaring consistency in each death was that Rose Veres held life insurance policies on each deceased resident. Rose was developing an incredible savings account from all the insurance policies cashed in.

The deaths in her boarding house began to draw the attention of the police. Rose was brought in for questioning a few times but no formal charges were ever filed. Why? There was no hard evidence linking her directly to their deaths and neighbors refused to testify.

She was, after all, a witch with powerful magic. The residents of Delray knew if she liked you, she could make the handsomest, smartest boy in the community fall in love with your daughter or make your sick child better. However, if she didn't like you, she would give you the evil eye in which case illness might fall upon your family or cause your husband to lose his job. So, they both respected and feared her powers and chose not to do anything that would cause her anger.

Indeed, Rose Veres made no secret of the fact she was a witch. She claimed to have been born with a full set of teeth and a caul over her face.[2] To the highly superstitious Hungarian community, these were an indication of someone born with strong supernatural powers.

---

2 A caul is a condition at birth where a portion of the birth membrane remains covering the face.

Rose boasted she knew all kinds of spells. Even if she was taken to jail, they could not keep her because Rose knew the magic to get out. Indeed, Rose had been taken in by the police on numerous occasions but always returned home.

She would walk up and down the streets with her black, flowing dress, dark flannel cape and hair cap. Neighbors would look away or stay behind closed doors. No matter what anyone said, the people knew with absolute certainty she was a witch with evil powers that could do anything.

It was a hot summer's day August 26, 1931. Young Marie Rose Chevalia was in the front yard of her house making mud pies. She kept a wary eye on the witch's house across the street.

For as far back as Marie Chevalia could remember, she had been warned about the woman who lived in the brown house across the street. As her mother and others had told her, behind the curtains of that home "… stalks a bad witch-woman. Her name is Mrs. Rose Veres. She bewitches factory-men. They go to live in her house. In the cellar the witch-woman brews potions. She has the Evil Eye. When she looks at these men, they have to do what she tells them. They want to go away but they can't. She bewitches them. Then they die."[3]

The little girl saw John Walker come outside the witch-woman's house. John was one of Rose Veres' boarders and an African American, one of several who had moved into the neighborhood over the past few years.

Marie watched as he began to water the lawn. Some time later the witch came out. The evil women who could turn into a wolf whenever she wanted.

Marie's attention was now fully focused on the witch. The little girl was prepared to run at a moment's notice. Marie heard Rose tell John Walker to stop what he was doing. At that, the man nodded, turned and went into the cellar to turn off the water. While he was gone, Marie saw Rose place a ladder against the house under a window. Another boarder, Steve Mak, came out with a toolbox and nails. Marie immediately noticed he was

---

3 *San Diego Union*, 3 April 1931, pg. 74.

not steady on his feet and fumbled with the toolbox as he ascended the ladder. By this time, John Walker had returned from the cellar and had come to watch.

MURDER HOUSE? This is the home of Veres at 7894 Medina street, where police cha have died under mysterious circumstances. See or was pushed from attic window in left wall.

Neighbors standing outside Rose Veres' home, waiting for her to return. (Detroit Free Press)

Mr. Mak reached the top and sat on the window ledge placing the toolbox beside him. Mak fumbled with the nail box, dropping its contents down. John Walker quickly covered his face, stepped away, and looked up.

It was then the little girl heard Mr. Mak moan, as if he were sick, then sway. The girl watched in absolute horror as Mr. Mak literally came flying from the window, striking the ground with an awful thud. She shrieked, looked up at the window and ran into her house.

It wasn't long after a crowd began to gather. Steve Mak was still alive, though barely. The ambulance arrived and rushed him to Detroit Receiving hospital where he would later die.

The fall was immediately considered suspicious. Rose swore to police it was an accident but a few neighbors' reports seem to dispute that claim. John Walker, Marie Chevalia, and a few others claimed to have seen Rose and her son, William, push Mak from the window. Rose was arrested.

The day of Rose Veres' arrest, the people of Delray gathered on the streets. The crowd remained until late into the night, waiting for the Witch of Delray to return.

An August 27, 1931 front page article in the Tyrone Daily Herald (a Pennsylvania newspaper) mentioned how the people watched the old house and whispered, "The witch lady is in jail again." The article described how the neighbors swore to the power of her abilities.

'She has strange powers,' they explained in a whisper. 'She boasts she cannot stay in jail and she knows the magic to get out.'

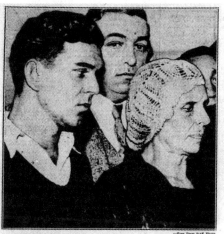

MRS. VERES AND SON ARRAIGNED. Mrs. Rose Veres and her son William are held in the County Jail without bail following their arraignment before Judge Henry S. Sweeny in Recorder's Court. A statement by the prosecutor's office that Mrs. Veres had confessed slaying Steve Mak, roomer in her home, later was challenged by her attorney.

Always before, the neighbors said, when there was trouble and she was arrested Mrs. Veres would return home—smiling grimly.

This time, however, she did not return.

Over 100 people were brought in for questioning, each begging not to be in the same room with her. One man

Rose Veres and her son William, arraigned. (Detail: Detroit Free Press, Sept. 1, 1931, pg. 30)

said, "She is dangerous. Look at her eyes. They go through you, they say such wicked things. I'm afraid for my job and for my family."[4]

Rose Veres herself went through intense interrogation by investigators. After more than 100 hours of brutal questioning, there was a break. Rose Veres confessed.

The man heading up this bizarre case was Wayne County Assistant Prosecutor, Duncan McCrea. It was McCrea who made the announcement to the newspapers.

In an article in the *The Coshocton Tribune* dated August 31, 1921, McCrea quoted the widow's confession:

---

4 Brown, Vera. "Witch Lady Prisoner in Detroit Jail." *Shamokin News-Dispatch [Shamokin, PA]* 28 Aug. 1931:6.

"I was hard up and needed the insurance money on the man. I tried to poison him twice but he didn't die, so I pushed him out of the attic window."

Shortly after Rose's so-called confession, a murder warrant was issued on her 18-year-old son, William. He was immediately arrested. Both Rose and William stood solemn and mute during arraignment. A plea of not guilty was entered on their behalf.

During this period, Rose Veres insisted she did not confess to any crime and that everything the prosecutor and police were saying was a lie. She said a paper had been put in front of her and police tried to force her to sign it. The investigators told her that her attorney was in jail and would remain there until she signed the paper. She didn't believe it. Rose swore she signed nothing.

When asked how the confession had been acquired, the prosecutor's office refused to reveal the details. Mrs. Veres' attorney continued to pressure McCrea. Eventually he came forward in a public announcement.

There was no signed document of guilt. Rose's so-called confession was only a verbal admission told to an individual who would remain "unnamed".

McCrea and his prosecution team continued to build evidence against Rose. A search of her home uncovered 75 life insurance policies of boarders or former boarders. All the insurance policies named her as beneficiary.

There was nothing wrong with that, Rose claimed. That's the way of her people. Rose said it was to cover any unpaid rent plus make sure a boarder got a good funeral. Indeed, Rose had done just that.

The trial started October 1, 1931. Of the nearly 100 people originally questioned by police, only a handful gave testimony. Each said it appeared Steve Mak had been pushed or thrown from the window by Rose Veres and her son, William.

One of the key witnesses was little Marie Chevalia who retold what she'd seen while making mud pies in her front yard. Next was John Walker, who had looked up into the window to see the face of Rose and her son. Walker additionally testified that Rose offered to pay him $500 if he wouldn't tell anyone what he'd seen.

The prosecution brought forward the fact that there had been up to twelve people who had died at Rose's boarding house in a seven year period. In each case, Rose was the sole beneficiary on their life insurance policies. Her attorney countered that claim by bringing the deputy coroner to testify. The coroner, who signed off on all deaths in the area, stated there was nothing unusual in that number of men dying within the specified time period. He also confirmed insurance policies usually were taken out for burial expenses by rooming home proprietors, like Rose.

A detective lieutenant with the Detroit Police Department took the stand for the prosecution. He stated Steve Mak had, the month before, been placed under partial police protection. This was the result of Mak being beaten in the basement of the home. The lieutenant further claimed, just a week before his death,

WITNESSES IN DEATH OF TENTH MAN. Rose Chevela and Catherine Zayak were questioned by police as witnesses in the death of Steve Mak, who fell or was pushed from an attic window of the Veres home. Mak's death led to investigation of nine other deaths.

Marie Rose Chevalia (left) was the child who witnessed the death from across the street and told police. (Detroit Free Press)

the police again visited the Veres' home to quiet a disturbance following the complaint of a neighbor.

The detective stated that Mak was upset, believing Mrs. Veres was trying to poison him so she could get his life insurance. However, as it would turn out, the coroner's report found no trace of poison in Mak's system and that actual cause of death was blunt-force trauma to the head.

The whole thing just gets more confusing from here. The blunt force trauma was more likely to have come from an object striking the head rather than a fall from a ladder. Had Mrs. Veres and her son again attempted to beat Mak to death? If he managed to survive the beating why in the world would he have stayed at the rooming home and why would he have so willingly gone up the ladder to fix a window?

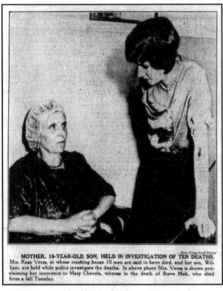

MOTHER, 18-YEAR-OLD SON, HELD IN INVESTIGATION OF TEN DEATHS. Mrs. Rose Veres, at whose rooming house 10 men are said to have died, and her son, William, are held while police investigate the deaths. In above photo Mrs. Veres is shown proclaiming her innocence to Mary Chavela, witness in the death of Steve Mak, who died from a fall Tuesday.

Rose Veres proclaims her innocence.
(Detroit Free Press)

After all the testimony was given, deliberation was short. The jury returned a verdict of guilty of murder in the first degree. During the verdict, Rose and William Veres remained unresponsive, void of emotion. The judge sentenced them both to life in prison. Rose went to the Detroit House of Corrections. Her son, William, was sent to Jackson State Prison.

When reporters asked Assistant Prosecutor Duncan McCrea about the powers of Rose Veres, he shook his head in disdain. She may have held the fears of the superstitious immigrant community but the fact was it was all just to keep the people on Medina Street quiet.

He did add, however, that Mrs. Veres seemed to have a strange, unexplainable power over the men at her lodging. He believed that was simply the men succumbing to their own superstitious beliefs and not the supernatural powers of Rose Veres.

McCrea added that the woman even attempted to give him and the investigators the evil eye. He admitted how some may be intimidated.

She would look steadily at you and point a finger. Her stare was intense, peculiar, almost hypnotic. There was something very strange about the whole thing. Supernatural powers? He did not buy that.

We should mention that, while in prison at the Detroit House of Corrections, Rose Veres was feared by most of the women inmates. Was it more superstition and ignorance or did Rose's power of intimidation and control extend beyond her Hungarian neighborhood?

This is usually where the story of the Witch of Delay ends. But, in this case, there's more to be told. Many believed that, although prison may have claimed her, her spell continued. A number of interesting events followed the imprisonment of Rose Veres and her son, William.

Two years after Rose had gone to prison, John Kempfl, a desperate former tenant and a man who had testified against Rose at the trial, went to the Detroit Police Department. He was frightened and pleaded with them to protect him, saying Rose Veres had cast a spell on him. Police sent him away, saying there was nothing they could do.

The next day John Kempfl cut his throat. It was only a superficial wound. The doctors said he would be fine but John said, "No. The witch cast her evil eye on me."[5] The next morning he was dead.

We attempted to follow the people who testified against Rose and William, particularly John Walker. Little Marie did grow up to live a good life. The others remain unknown, even John Walker. The name was very common.

Something interesting did happen to the well-respected Assistant Prosecuting Attorney, Duncan McCrea, who led the prosecution against Rose. He was responsible for misrepresenting to the public her signed confession of guilt, a confession he attempted to coerce her into signing. Rose blamed him for twisting the facts to make her look guilty and blamed him for her imprisonment. As previously mentioned, the witch had cursed him along with the Detroit Police Department for their actions. A curse that McCrea had laughed off.

---

5 "Nemesis of Detroit Witch Dies Blaming Her Evil Eye." *Detroit Free Press.* 9 May 1933: 1.

In the immediate years that followed, Duncan McCrea was given acco-lades for his excellent prosecutorial work and was elected Prosecuting At-torney of Wayne County. His reputation as a fearless prosecutor became more prominent shortly after Rose and William's conviction. His political star was rising and he was seriously considering a run for senator.

To help boost his political strength as a fearless fighter of corruption, in the 1930's he went after a white Aryan supremacist group known as the Black Legion. This highly secret undercover group was believed to be behind many murders, attempted murders, and fire bombings throughout Michigan.

Little did McCrea know his career would soon come tumbling down and his image irreversibly damaged. In 1934, it would be revealed that Mc-Crea himself was a member of the Black Legion. He disputed the claims vehemently, until an affidavit of enrollment was presented with his signa-ture on it.

Things went from bad to worse. He would also become involved in one of Detroit's largest racketeering scandals. It would not only bring him down but also a huge portion of the Detroit Police Department. Most of them were involved in Rose and William Veres' conviction.

Investigators, officers and department leaders were fired or prosecuted for racketeering. That included Duncan McCrea.

McCrea's trial led to his conviction. With sentencing delays and other legal bantering, he did not begin serving his term until 1943. McCrea was sent to Jackson Prison, ironically the same prison where William Veres was serving his life term. One of the first to greet McCrea as he entered Jackson Prison was William Veres.

Meanwhile, Rose's neighbors in Delray had banded together and were raising funds to help with Rose and William's retrial. They believed the verdict brought in by the jurors in Recorder's Court, Judge Thomas Cotter's courtroom, was grossly unjust.

A new defense attorney agreed to take up the cause for Rose and William's case and aggressively moved forward with an appeal and retrial.

Her name was Alena B. Clutts. She was a well-respected, highly skilled Detroit attorney and, after reviewing Rose and William's trial transcripts and doing some preliminary investigations, also believed a gross injustice had occurred.

Mrs. Clutts cleaned up the debris of misinformation and twisted facts presented by McCrea's prosecution team. Through her competent management of the facts related to the case and her knowledge of law, she won a retrial for both William and Rose. William's retrial took place in 1944. He was found not guilty. We can only imagine the regret McCrea felt as he watched William Veres walk past his cell a free man.

In 1945 came Rose's retrial. The day the verdict was read, the courtroom was filled to capacity with current and former residents of Delray. When "not guilty" was announced, the courtroom exploded in applause. Rose openly wept. The jury, when later questioned by news reporters, claimed that Rose was clearly not guilty and stated they couldn't understand how any jury would have ever convicted her.

After 14 very long years, Rose and William were finally free. Rose went to live with her youngest son. She lived a peaceful life, eventually dying from natural causes in her late 70's. Her son, William, married. The couple started a family and moved far away from Delray and its dark memories.

Rose always said she knew the magic to get out of prison. Was it Rose's magic powers that released her and her son or simply the act of a dedicated attorney who believed Rose and William had been done an injustice? As far as Prosecutor McCrea and members of the Detroit Police Department, were their fates sealed by their own greed and corruption, or was it the Wiccan's Creed and the curse of the Delray Witch?

ALIMIPEGON

On ne connoit point le Cours de toutes ces Rivieres.

PARTIE OCCIDENTALE
de la
NOUVELLE FRANCE
ou du
CANADA
Par Mr. Bellin Ingenieur du Roy et de la
Pour servir à l'Intelligence des Affaires et de
present en Amerique, communiquée au Publi
les Heritiers de Homan, en l'an 1755.
Echelles
Lieues Communes de France de 25. au T
Lieues Marines de France et d'Angleterre de 20.

Baye de Michipicoton

Isle Maurepas

C. Chailley

Ance aux Sables

I. Pontchartrain

Cap Hoquart

Minabaujou

I. Hocquare

Ilots S.t Gilles

R. aux Testes Boules

Hayre Beauharnois

R. Beauharnois

I.S.t Anne

Beauharnois

R. a Charon

R. au Galop

Mamene

Toute cette coste n'est pas connue

La GrandeIsle

Baye de Bachouanan

R. Bachunan

Pointe des Chenes

LES SAUTEURS

Marie

Isle Manitoulin

Mission Marie

Pointe aux Thessalons

Fort et Mission abandonnée

S.t Michillimakinac

aux Bois Blanc

Ance au Tonerre

LAC HURON

Baye des Noquets

I. du Castor

I.S. Ioseph

LAC MICHIGAN

R. aux Busoies

R. A'Oulamanitou

R. du P.r Marquet

R. S.t Nicolas

R. aux Sable

Baye de Seguinam

ANCIEN PAYS DES HURONS

R. Blanche

Portage

R. Mahican

La Grande Riviere

la Belle Chasse

R. au Raisin

Village Missisagué

Riviere Inconnu à tous les
remonte 80 Lieues sans trou

R. a la Barbue

Village de Boutenatami

Port. Pontchartrain

LAC S.t CLAIRE

Village
Outnaes

LES SAKIS

Mission de S.t
Francois Xavier
Lac

R. Marameg

R. Noir

et Port de Checagou

Village de Narouas

Detroit

I. des Serpens Sonnettes

Pelee

LAC ER

Collins

Village de Miamis

R.S. Ioseph

des Miamis

Toute cette coste n'est presque p

Portage des Chenes

Village de Boutenatami

Le Fort
Sources Portage
du Theakiki

Sources de
la Riviere
Ouabache

PAYS DES MIAMIS

PAYS DES

Qui ont été detruit par de

R. de Theakiki

R. Chisagou

R. Chisago

R. Ouabache ou S.t Jerome

S.t Jerome

Oyo ou la Belle Riviere

Ch

Eternal Retribution of the Sauk

Flint, MI

Long before the white man settled in Michigan there were stories shared among the indigenous people and quietly spoken in small circles and around evening campfires. It is a story of war, spiritual revenge and eternal retribution.

Many believe stories of the Sauk annihilation are myth, a legend passed through the centuries by Chippewa, Ottawa and Ojibwa. There is nothing written on paper nor proof that such an extermination occurred in Michigan. Yet, the stories persist and the old ones swear it is true. Be vigilant. The Sauk spirits are near.

Let us go back in time to the 17th century. Michigan was a land of wilderness consisting of dense forests, vast grassy plains, clear waters, and abundant wildlife.

This story comes from a very old Chieftain named Puttasamine. The stories of Puttasamine were recounted in several journals. The interview was originally conducted in 1834 and translated by Peter Gruette, described as a "half-breed".

At the time of the interview, Puttasamine claimed to be at least 100 years old. The story was told to him by his grandfather who, at the time of that telling, was also thought to be at least 100.

Photo opposite: 1755 Map of the Great Lakes (public domain)

In those earlier years of Michigan, Sauk claimed the eastern Lower Peninsula of the state. At their strongest, Sauk villages could be found along Lake Michigan North of Petoskey and south of Bay City into Macomb County. Their main village, however, was along the west side of the Saginaw River (Saug-an-te-nah-ke-wat or Sāginā'we', meaning place where the Sauk were or place of the Sauk).

"Ne Sou A Quoit," 1842, from History of the Indian Tribes of North America, Creator Unknown (used with permission, Southern Methodist University, DeGolyer Library)

Sauk were Algonquin-speaking people and their appearance said to be distinctive. Warriors traditionally wore their hair Mohawk style or shaved their heads completely, leaving only a scalplock (one long lock of hair on top of the head). Occasionally they would add porcupine quills to make it more impressive.

The Sauk were not liked by other tribes. They were aggressive, war-mongers, vicious, and cruel. It was not uncommon for them to invade other villages, mercilessly killing the people. Chippewa and Ottawa decided it was time to stop the attacks and called a great council of the People.

So it was, around 1634, a nation of tribes were secretly summoned to Mackinac Island. Chieftains and tribal leaders from Wisconsin and Michigan down to the six nations of New York converged on the island. After days of powwow, a war of extermination was decided. It would begin in the heart of Sauk territory, the Saginaw Valley.

Hidden by the darkness of night, Chippewa warriors quietly made their way by canoes down the shores of Lake Huron until they arrived at a place approximately 10 miles above the mouth of the Saginaw River. At that point, some disembarked and traveled by land while others continued their journey to the east bank of the Saginaw.

The attack came with the power of a cyclone, taking the Sauk by complete surprise. It was brutal. The Sauk people were slaughtered—nearly every man, woman and child. According to legend, the destruction was so great the rivers flowed red with Sauk blood.

A few warriors escaped into the wilderness. It is believed they retreated to the Grand River and down that stream to Lake Michigan.

Other Sauk took canoes and crossed the river to another island on the east side. Those who escaped thought they were safe, knowing the invaders did not have canoes. However, the waters froze, the ice became thick and the warriors advanced.

The Sauk took a final stand, not giving up their island refuge easily. It was a hopeless battle. They were greatly outnumbered but they fearlessly fought to the very end.

In later years the extent of carnage would be discovered. A huge number of skulls along with remaining bones were uncovered on the island. Legend has it that the land where this massacre occurred would become known as Skull Island.

After the Chippewa's first battle by the Saginaw River, they proceeded to villages along the Shiawassee, Tittabawassee, Cass and northern Flint River. During this time, Ottawa came from the south and destroyed villages at the southern end of the Flint River.

Accounts say the battles may have moved as far south as the banks of the Clinton River in Macomb County and northwest, to Lake Michigan. Eventually, all Sauk were gone or destroyed except for twelve women.

Stories regarding the fate of the twelve surviving women vary. Some say they were brutalized and eventually tortured to death. Others say they were given mercy and sent west of the Mississippi to the Sioux people who promised to care for them. It is said the Sioux held true to their promise.

After the battles were over, Chippewa and Ottawa tribes became absolute masters of Sauk country. The former lands of the Sauk were divided into common hunting ground. Peace settled over the land. Until, that is, the men of the villages began to disappear. They would leave to hunt, as they had for many years, but this time they did not return.

The first few who disappeared were thought to have encountered a fatal accident, which happened during hunts. However, when the numbers of missing grew, frightened whispers began.

Some wondered if the Sauk who had escaped during the massacres remained in the woodlands and were picking them off. Men stopped going off by themselves to hunt, instead deciding to form hunting parties. If there were remaining Sauk hiding in the woods, they would be destroyed like all the others.

Sauk War Dance, ca. 1842 (Southern Methodist University, DeGolyer Library)

It wasn't long before stories started coming back more powerful, more fearful than any associated with flesh and blood Sauk warriors. Indeed, hunting parties returned claiming visions of Sauk spirits roaming the dense forests.

Fear grew. The Manesous (bad spirits) were hovering. Fear quickly turned to obsession as visions of Sauk spirits were seen everywhere. Manesous were in the immediate vicinity! So great was their anxiety that some rushed from villages, leaving behind wigwams, fish, game and camp equipment. No one could convince them that their visions were in error.

Their belief in the Manesous continued for many years. Accounts from early explorers and trappers to Michigan say their Ottawa, Ojibwa, and Potawatomi guides refused to enter the former lands of the Sauk, believing the area was haunted by their vengeful spirits. It was called the Forbidden Valley. This area did not just include Saginaw Bay but also areas extending westward to Grand River Valley.

As a result of their fear of the Forbidden Valley, Native American guides would avoid the area entirely, taking white explorers around Michigan's thumb. Even into the 1850's some of the older Native Americans in the southeastern counties of Michigan believed Manesous remained in the woodlands seeking revenge on those who caused their annihilation. Eventually time, like the ever-moving waters of the river, washed away fear of Manesous and Native Americans returned to the land.

Although there were certainly battles among the indigenous people of Michigan, the story of Sauk extermination remains a legend. Some consider it pure myth.

Yet, a mystery lingers over the land today. Although many people living in the Forbidden Valley may not have heard stories of the Sauk massacre, there are stories of unexplainable things going on in the area, especially around the woodlands and rivers.

Murphy Lake State Park in Millington is one area where numerous accounts of strange activity have been reported. Voices and muffled screams are heard when hikers are alone on the trails. Of course, sound carries easily in the dense forest. It's certainly possible the voices are other living hikers unseen in the park. Yet that doesn't account for the moans and voices that some swear are very close to them, within a few yards of where they stand.

There have been other reports, of course. Vague, shimmering images distorting the trees and shrubbery for a brief moment. Dark shadows, some close enough to momentarily block the light from your vision. Even more stories exist of glowing lights moving through the woods at night. Then there are the creatures, described as half human, half animal, with bright green eyes that wander the area in and around Murphy Lake State Park and the hills of Millington.

Skull Island is another mysterious spot. This is the place, south of Bay City and east of the Saginaw River, where legend states the Sauk took their last stand. Long ago there were reports of trappers and early settlers claiming to hear cries, shouts and women weeping when they were alone. There is one account of a trapper who ran in fear, believing someone unseen pursued him. What spirits, if any, remain on Skull Island? A number of years back, the area was purchased and is privately owned. It is no longer open to the public. If spirits linger they remain in quiet, undisturbed solitude. Perhaps this is as it should be.

We may never know the truth behind the Sauk massacre. The facts and truth are lost to time. Yet, are there clues today that may lead us to a conclusion?

Recently, a woman recalled a time in the early 1950's when she attended school in Flushing. Sometimes she and her friends would skip classes. They often headed to Mill Street near Flushing Road to look for arrowheads. She claimed arrowheads were everywhere back then. The girls didn't really think about the significance of the arrowheads, they just enjoyed the search. After finding one, they'd toss it out onto the street and continue on their exploration.

One of the big battles took place in the Flushing area. Were these massive amounts of arrowheads a confirmation of that battle?

In January of 2008, a construction crew was clearing out an area of land on the 500 block of Stone Street in Flint for development of a government housing project. While digging out the basement of an old home, human remains were uncovered. It turned out to be ancient Native American remains.

Demolition ceased and a team of archeologists and members of the Saginaw Chippewa Indian Tribe began an excavation, eventually uncovering an estimated 88 bodies. The age of the dead ranged from infants and young children to teenagers and adults. None showed evidence of ill health. Analysis is still not complete, but the early results suggest the bones were all well over 1,000 years old, very possibly much older.

This discovery is not the only such find in Flint. Other Native American remains were uncovered at M-15 and Bristol Road in Flint in the summer of 1962. It is also thought more Native American remains exist around Atwood Stadium and other locations in the area. There is much discussion going on as far as whether widespread excavation should be conducted. What has been discovered? Was it simply an ancient Indian burial site or is it something more?

In a 1905 book that included articles by different unknown authors and edited by Charles A. Lippincott, an account of a major Sauk battle is described. The article stated it was the biggest battle of the war and occurred on a high bluff overlooking the Flint River. This 1905 writing further pinpointed the site of the battle being directly across the river from the School for the Deaf. As it turns out, Stone Street is on a bluff overlooking the Flint River and directly across the river is the Michigan School for the Deaf.

In our many travels and investigations over the past 10 years, we've uncovered the truth behind many urban legends. What we've learned is that within each legend there lies an element of truth. Is that the case with the great Sauk massacres? Do Manesous still roam? Perhaps the Forbidden Valley is haunted and reports of apparitions and voices in Murphy Lake State Park true.

As the old ones say, "Be vigilant. The Sauk spirits are near."

Lost Boy
of Mackinac Island

From 2011 and 2014 my sister, Bev Rydel, and I held a series of public weekend investigations called "A Haunted Weekend on Mackinac Island." During the weekend we would conduct a series of day- and night-time investigations at various locations. Stories of the most active investigations are contained in our book, *Haunted Travels of Michigan III: Spirits Rising*. The following account, however, occurred after our third book was released. It would turn out to be one of the most emotionally compelling moments in our many island investigations.

We first heard the little boy on October 8, 2011. It was an unseasonably warm and beautiful fall day. Daytime investigations had just ended at our first Haunted Weekend on Mackinac Island. Bev and I had a few hours before the evening investigations began and decided to take a leisurely walk along the water.

We headed north on Lake Shore Drive, leaving Mission Point Resort in the early afternoon. Within a few minutes we found ourselves at the base of the stairway leading up to Arch Rock.

Bev and I were in one of our quiet moments, each with our own thoughts. That's when I heard a voice. Faint,

Photo opposite: Carriage tours take visitors past Sugar Loaf Rock. (Kathleen Tedsen)

almost imperceptible, yet still audible. It was higher pitched, like a child's voice. The voice sounded distressed. I couldn't understand what it said.

Bev stopped, her eyes looking up toward the familiar vision of Arch Rock. She had heard it, too.

I said, "Was it a child's voice?"

"I thought so," was her response.

"Could you understand what it said?"

Bev shook her head. "No."

We stood there for several minutes but didn't hear the child's voice again or, for that matter, any voices. Knowing Arch Rock was one of the island's most popular tourist attractions, Bev and I dismissed the voice, believing it was probably a child with his family. We continued our walk, not knowing that anomalous little voice would be heard again.

Our first encounter with the lost boy during a walk along the lake near Arch Rock. (Kathleen Tedsen)

We returned to the island the next year. Part of our 2012 daytime investigations took us to a location we call "Death Trail". It's located a few miles from downtown Mackinac on a small dirt trail not far from Arch Rock. It was believed a former student of Mackinac College might have committed suicide in this area.

For those unfamiliar, Mackinac College was the island's first and only college. It was a private school led by Peter Howard, who was a dedicated member of the Moral Re-Armament (MR-A). The MR-A was a religious movement that some considered a cult.

The college's lifespan was rather short, operating from just 1966 to 1970. Winters are very harsh on the island and travel to the mainland is difficult. This kept Mackinac College students tied to the island. With little to do besides study, enrollment declined. It was decided the expense of keeping the college running could not sustain the low enrollments. It closed in 1970.

Craig was a student at Mackinac College during its operation, and it was he who committed suicide. He was a relatively quiet young man. On a cold February day in 1967 he left the college for a hike and never returned. Search parties went out but were unable to find him.

It wasn't until the following summer two young boys riding their bicycles on a remote trail near Arch Rock discovered his body. It appeared the student had killed himself with a rifle or shotgun (the gun went missing). There was a cryptic message pinned to his jacket that said something about him going back to his planet.

The reason for the suicide is unclear. Some believe he went crazy; others think he was depressed over a broken relationship. Yet others say another student might have murdered him.

Because of that mystery and the surprising and tragic death of Craig, we decided to make a daytime trip to Death Trail in the hope of making a spiritual contact with the student. Perhaps he would provide an answer to his death.

Our small group wandered down the narrow dirt trail, brushing past trees, shrubs and overgrown brush as we made our way further into the heavily wooded area. Up to this point the electromagnetic field levels (EMF)[1] were flat. That quickly changed as a female member of the group called out a sudden spike in EMF levels. We stopped.

---

1 EMF (electromagnetic fields) meter. Electromagnetic fields are part of earth's atmosphere. Everything on earth generates some level of EMF. It is believed, in the paranormal community, when a spirit energy or some type of continued consciousness enters a room or an area and wishes to communicate, it will disrupt or increase the EMF levels as it draws energy to communicate. It is hoped EMF meters will pick up those EMF elevations, signaling a possible communication.

Bev and I brought our EMF meters to the area where the woman stood. We quickly saw her KII meter flashing wildly. Our own EMF meters confirmed hers with elevations shooting up as we neared her location.

The woman from our group thought it might be a child since the high EMF elevations began at the ground and stopped between three or four feet above the ground.

Arch Rock has been one of Mackinac Island's favorite tourist attractions for over a century. (Kathleen Tedsen)

The meters traced a vortex of energy that fell within a small circular area. I watched the hair on the back of my arms rise and felt a sudden lightheadedness, my body's typical response to high EMF levels. This remote, wooded area was holding a strong energy field.

When asked if it was a child, the EMF immediately rose higher, signaling a possible response. EMF levels remained unresponsive when I asked if there was a man or women present.

Bev then asked the validation question. "Children? Are there children here?" The meter immediately responded. It was then we captured a child's voice on our audio recorder that said "Hello." What followed that small voice was a series of EMF responses to questions.

Based on EMF hits and the small recorded voice, it seemed we were communicating with a child who had been with his mother and father. Some type of accidental, violent encounter had happened and the mother and father died.

We asked what had happened to the child. It was then the EMF levels dropped and the charged atmosphere dissipated. If any conscious energy had been near us, it was gone.

We hadn't yet equated this brief encounter with the child's voice we'd heard in 2011 near Arch Rock. That wouldn't come to mind until the following year.

We continued with the afternoon's session, mentally filing away that particular moment as one of the more interesting but unidentifiable phenomena on the island. We knew it would be nearly impossible to do any viable research with only a child's "Hello" recorded.

October 5, 2013 was our next Haunted Weekend on the island. The daytime investigations culminated at Arch Rock. After our carriages dropped us off, they left.

It had been a cold, rainy morning and the ground was soaked. It was very cool but at least the wind was gone. Because of the inclement weather, the general tourist population stayed away and we found ourselves pretty much alone.

After a few uneventful, random EVP[2] sessions many in our group wandered back to the hotel to warm up and rest. That left Bev and I with a small group of six or seven. Unknown to us, those of us who stayed were about to have one of the most emotionally powerful moments of all our Mackinac Island investigations.

We began our final afternoon EVP questions. Each member of our group held either a KII or Mel meter to register fluctuations in EMF. We began by calling out for Craig, the suicidal Mackinac College student, to come forward. The EMF meters remained flat, unresponsive. Unknown to us, things were about to change.

We heard voices down the trail. Our group grew quiet and stepped off the pathway, allowing the visitors to pass. Soon a young couple with a baby in

---

2 EVP (electronic voice phenomena) Session. An EVP is believed to be the voice of a spirit. The sound is too low to be heard by ear but can be recorded on an audio recorder. Later, the audio file can be loaded into an audio editing software program and adjustments made to hear the voice. An EVP Session is a series of questions asked to elicit a response.

a stroller passed us. We returned smiles and nods. There was clearly a question in their eyes as they looked at our small group and the unusual-looking devices held in our hands. They didn't ask what we were doing and we didn't share as they moved on, heading toward Arch Rock.

It was within a few seconds of their passing that the EMF meters started going off. Levels instantly shot up with all five lights of our KII meters flashing rapidly. We came to attention. Perhaps something or someone had come to visit.

Had the young family kicked up some type of spirit or conscious energy? A few general questions were asked without EMF response. A member of our group wondered if a child had joined us. We watched with interest as the EMF meter in the woman's hand instantly spiked. Even more interesting, the meters held in each member's hands began to go off. The meter's light would wildly flash and go off as the next person's meter spiked. It swept around us several times, one after the other until all our meters were going off.

Our group exchanged questioning glances. What did we have here?

I asked if whatever was with us liked children. The EMF meters showed another strong energy spike.

One of the women wondered if it was a child spirit who had joined us, thinking the energy may have been stimulated by the passing baby and young parents. EMF levels made a brief, imperceptible jump.

I asked again if a child was with us. This time the meter spiked. Not just one but several devices registered in the group with the same swirling sweep of activity.

"Are you a little boy?" I asked and again the KII meter registered all five lights. Levels flattened when I asked if it was a girl. For validation, I again asked if it was a boy and the KII meters responded.

Okay. This was getting interesting.

We tried to determine the child's age. I covered several age ranges without EMF response. Then came my next question, "Young man, are you under five years old?"

EMF levels went crazy. Their continuous, rapid pulsing spikes suggested whatever was around us was very excited, generating massive amounts of energy. If we were, in fact, communicating with a child spirit perhaps he was excited to know we were able to communicate with him.

I attempted to calm him down and asked him to step away for a moment. It took several attempts before the levels finally flattened.

"Can you tell us your name?" The KII meter lights fluttered weakly then went dark.

I asked why the child remained on the island. This time there was absolutely no EMF elevation.

I asked if he were born on the island. Still no response. Had he been visiting the island? Again, no EMF elevation.

It's as if the child was confused, unsure of the answer. Perhaps he simply didn't remember or know. If it was a spirit energy with us, perhaps its strength was waning.

I paused for a moment then continued, "Did you die on the island?"

Something very curious happened at that moment. A strong wind began to rise. It moved through the trees, pushing its way through dry autumn leaves, causing a riot of sound like thousands of fingernails tapping against a window. It rushed downward towards our group and stilled at the very moment the EMF meters came alive. The meters went off in a blast, their lights moving from one investigator's device to another. Again the sweeping surge of energy encircled us.

I asked if he was afraid. The EMF levels sharply rose before settling down again. I told him not to be afraid. It may seem a little frightening with all of us standing close together but we would do nothing to hurt him.

Wind shifted through the dry autumn leaves as it again descended on our group. There was a noticeable shift in the atmosphere. The telltale signs of hair rising on the back of my arms and that lightheaded feeling told me EMF levels were high.

If felt very much like it had during our investigation the previous year on Death Trail. As if she knew what I was thinking, Bev pulled me away from the group.

"Remember last year on Death Trail?" She asked.

"I was just thinking that. The child again?"

Bev nodded, "It's a possibility." She then reminded me of the child's voice we heard in this same area back in 2011. I had forgotten about that. That's when Bev and I considered the possibility this child spirit may have been trying to communicate with us for a few years. We returned to the group.

"Are you lost, little boy? Are you looking for your mom and dad?" With that, the EMF levels shot up with KII meters responding to the change. The levels remained high for a second or two before leveling off.

We exchanged glances. Sadness pulled at our hearts. Had we really encountered the frightened spirit of a lost boy?

"How did you lose your mom and dad? Did they die?" EMF levels immediately elevated then subsided.

Remembering the EVP session with a little child from last year and the response to questions related to his mother and father being killed, I asked, "Did they have an accident?" EMF levels rose, then fell and elevated again when asked if they had fallen from a big rock.

I asked if he was alone. Again, strong EMF elevations seemed to confirm the question.

Tears glistened along the edges of Bev's eyes as she said, "This is so sad." The others nodded in agreement. We all grew silent.

Bev asked, "Did you fall off of Arch Rock, sweetie?" The increase of EMF levels suggested he had.

A women in the group whispered, "I'm really feeling it right here." Indeed, the atmosphere had become heavy, charged in the area in front of her. The hand that held the flashing KII meter slightly trembled as she glanced at me.

I wondered if we could cross this little one over. I would try to send him into the light.

"Do you know how to get back to your mom and dad?" I asked. "Do you want us to help you find them?" Another EMF response.

"Alright, let's see if we can help you find them. If you look carefully, you're going to see a white light." The KII meters flashed briefly. I had this sense the child was uncertain.

"Yes you will," I said. KII meter lights flashed a confirmation.

"You've seen it?" Again the KII meter's lights rapidly flashed.

Second encounter with the lost boy on Death Trail not far from Arch Rock, 2012. (Kathleed Tedsen and Beverlee Rydel)

"I want you to go into that light. Don't be afraid, honey, because that's where mom and dad are." The EMF levels rose, lightly fluctuating, before leveling off.

"That's where mom and dad are and they're waiting for you but you have to cross over. You have to go through the light. It's not scary. I know you're probably afraid but it's not scary. In fact, you're going to be so happy once you get into that light. Would you do that for us now?" KII meters quickly flashed full red.

"Just go into the light, honey. You'll find them. They're there waiting for you. They've been there all along. Go into the light, honey. Go. Be happy. Be happy."

Throughout this time, I watched as the EMF levels increased and fluctuated with each comment or question.

I continued. "Will you do that for us? Will you go into the light?"

It was then I believe the transition began. Suddenly, EMF levels on the devices of those around me flattened. Only the meter held by the woman who had originally sensed the young spirit continued to pulse. The energy clung to her as the meter she held continued to flash. Perhaps the little boy had found some spiritual connection or comfort from this woman. He stubbornly stayed with her.

"Go into the light. Don't be afraid," I encouraged.

"You have to go into that white light. It's not scary at all. Mom and dad are there. They're waiting. Go in peace. Don't stay here any more. Don't stay here any more. Go into the light."

For a few seconds the EMF levels on the device held by the woman flattened. We were silent, vigilant, hoping the boy had transitioned. Then I saw the woman's KII lights again flash. He was still hanging on to her.

"I know you're probably afraid. I know. You've probably been here a long time, haven't you? I know you're looking for your mother and father. Well, how you find them is by going into that light that you see. That's the only way."

The KII light grew weaker. I pulled on the power of God and faith.

"Do you believe in God?" I asked. The meter's light quickly flashed. I took that as a confirmation.

"Well guess what, in that light you'll not only find your parents, you'll see God. Just go. You won't be afraid any more. I promise ... if you believe in God ... and a greater power."

With those words, a sudden burst of wind came. The movement of the wind was very unusual. It seemed to originate from the very ground around us. It circled our feet, then our legs as it ascended. The wind rapidly moved into the trees, sending leaves into a wild dance, tearing a few from branches. The falling leaves scattered around us; we all stood silent, mesmerized. We thought it was over but not quite. The meter in the woman's hand still fluttered. It was very weak. It was still holding on to her energy. I asked her to directly encourage the transition.

She responded, "Go into the light, honey. See your mom and dad. They're there."

With those final words, the meter's lights faded and EMF elevations stopped. Whatever had been with us was gone.

We looked at one another. Had we really just crossed over the spirit of a young boy? It was a remarkable moment.

There was no question this had been quite an emotional session. However, Bev and I remained somewhat skeptical about whether a cross-over had actually happened. Even as compelling as the consistent EMF responses were and even the remarkable burst of wind at the end followed by the dropping of EMF elevations, we stubbornly would not admit a cross-over.

Bev and I know EMF meters are extremely fallible. They can and do respond to natural, atmospheric waves and to electronic devices, like cell phones. Because of that, Bev and I don't use them alone as confirmation of a paranormal event. We have to validate it with something recorded. We both agreed, we would need to be very diligent when listening to this audio and doing research.

History, of course, is key in validating a paranormal event. Of course, we knew finding historical records associated with the death of a man, woman and/or child somewhere near Arch Rock at some unknown time in the island's history would be like finding a strand of hair in the ocean. Indeed, the island's history is quite vast and much of it unknown.

According to records, the first Native Americans arrived around 900 A.D. and European travelers came 700 years later. Much of those early years and the centuries that followed remain undocumented. We hoped the deaths, if this event even happened, occurred in the late 19th century when better records were kept.

As research began, we quickly uncovered an interesting story of Native American tradition associated with Arch Rock. The indigenous people believed Arch Rock served as the gateway or entry of Gitchie Manitou (Great Spirit) and the fairies. Upon entering this realm, Gitchie Manitou and the fairies made their way to Sugar Loaf, a 75 ft. cone-shaped monolithic limestone rock that shoots straight up from the ground. It was Sugar Loaf where Manitou and the fairies made their home.

Because Great Spirit entered through Arch Rock, it was considered a most sacred place. It is believed that Arch Rock was the location where earth-bound souls left the earth on their transition to the other realm. That would make the transition of our lost boy easier. Perhaps that was why the lost boy was there? He was ready to transition and we helped him through.

As research continued, we failed to find any historical reference to the death of a man or child near Arch Rock. We did, however, find a small article in the Jackson Citizen Patriot newspaper dated October 23, 1877.

In that article, it described an early 1800's visitor who wanted to explore the island's back roads. He followed guides to a place called Fairy Arch. We discovered that Fairy Arch is located just south of Arch Rock and has some resemblance to the bigger rock formation.

While at Fairy Arch, one of the guides spotted something unusual poking out of the rocky terrain. He removed some of the loose rocks and discovered human remains. The remains appeared to be that of a young woman. Her body had been doubled up and stuffed in a crevice then purposefully covered with large stones and earth. Over the years, the earth washed away, exposing the bones.

It was believed she had been murdered. This conclusion came because Fairy Arch, at that time in Mackinac Island history, was a very remote location. Only a few islanders knew about its existence. It was thought whoever put her body there believed no one would discover it. Adding to suspicion of murder was the unnatural position of the body and the attempt at covering it up.

Who was this young woman and what happened to her? It was never known and remains one of the island's many mysteries.

Could this young woman be connected to the child? If the location had been more thoroughly excavated, would they have discovered the remains of a man and child? Could those remains still be undiscovered at Fairy Arch?

Bev and I set up the audio of our time at Arch Rock and very carefully listened to the last 30 minutes. Nothing unusual was heard. We were at the final moments of the session. We pressed the headphones close and heard the wind begin to rise.

There was a sound. A voice. Bev said nothing just looked at me as she pulled out the short clip, reduced white noise and enhanced audio levels. There it was. A child's voice. One word, "Papa."

The lost boy of Mackinac Island had finally gone home.

Note: The entire video recording of this session can be found on our website www.hauntedtravelsmi.com/stepping

Murder House

This is not a story for the squeamish. It is dark and disturbing, like a horrible nightmare but quite true.

Is there a trigger in each of us? Something…some event or series of events, a person we know, or perhaps an unseen force that will, without notice, draw out our inner demon? Something that awakens whatever has been sleeping inside us for years. Once it's out, it can't be controlled. We do something beyond what we thought we were ever capable of doing. We do something so dreadful, our life loses meaning and we wake up in hell. This is such a story.

Mt. Vernon, Michigan in 1889 was a small farming community lying between Romeo and Washington Township. William Major was a farmer in Mt. Vernon and, with a large piece of land, considered one of the area's more well-to-do citizens.

His family consisted of his wife, Mary, about 10 years his junior, and their three living children, Sarah, Pheobe, and their son, Jesse. In 1874, their youngest boy, William, Jr., at the tender age of four, died during a scarlet fever epidemic that took out many children in the area. It had been a terrible time for William and Mary but they both moved forward, knowing that death was part of life.

Photo opposite: Depiction of triple murder (Used with permission, National Police Gazette)

The life of a farmer wasn't easy but William never feared hard work. It had always been a part of his life from as far back as he could remember. Sometimes, however, the work got a little harder. Especially when he got the Fever. Somewhere, perhaps in the war, he had contracted the Fever. It came and went. One day he'd be fine and the next it would hit. He'd struggled through it most times because farming didn't always allow a man to be sick. There were, however, times when it hit him so hard he'd have to lay low until it subsided.

The Fever wasn't the only thing he'd brought back from the war. There were memories. The Civil War was just about the most God-awful thing he had experienced. William enlisted in June of 1863 and served in Michigan's 8th Calvary. He'd seen things and done things that no man should have to see or do. It had hardened him. He came out a different man than the one he was when he went in. But that was a quarter century ago. He didn't let it drag on him anymore. At least, that's what he told himself.

William's wife, Mary, was a decent woman, he supposed. She took good care of the house and the children and her cooking was good enough. Still, she was damned strong-willed and didn't always do what he wanted. They knocked heads and he had to put her in her place a time or two. What marriage is perfect?

He also had a problem with his daughter, Pheobe. She didn't listen. Like her mamma, she was strong-headed. A little too wild by his mind.

A few years back, Phoebe ran off and married an immigrant from Germany. The marriage was very short-lived, ending in divorce. She had nowhere to go but back home. She was very unhappy and her father was angry. According to Phoebe, he had threatened to kill her if she did something stupid like that again. Depressed over the whole situation, she took poison, attempting to kill herself. Fortunately, Mary got her to a doctor in time and she was saved. Since then, Phoebe spent a lot of time with friends.

Truth was, the only one in the family William took a liking to was his then 14-year old son, Jesse. Having lost his first son years back, he couldn't do enough for Jesse. Although Jesse would later admit he was afraid of his father.

The Christmas of 1889 was a pretty normal one for the Major family. Their oldest daughter, Sarah, her husband, Charles Joseph (Joe) Depew, and their three-year old grandbaby, Maudie, had come to visit. After Christmas, Joe had to return to work so he headed back to Ortonville, leaving Sarah and their daughter with her family.

On the morning of December 28, they awoke to a beautiful, sunny day and William suggested the family head into Romeo for a day of shopping

Map of Romeo, Michigan, ca. 1868. (Courtesy Library of Congress)

and socializing. They were excited by that opportunity. William hitched up the horses and they piled into the wagon. It was a joyful ride as they chatted and laughed on their way into town.

Once they reached Romeo, William told Mary he had a short errand and would be right back. He met up with them not long after and they continued their cheerful day in town.

When it was time to leave, Phoebe mentioned there was a dance in Romeo that night and she wanted to stay. She would spend the night at her friend's home. The family agreed and said goodbye, returning home with a few packages in hand.

William dropped off his family at the farm and headed over to William and Elizabeth Gulick's place. The Gulicks were Mary's elderly parents who lived about a quarter mile away. William had promised to fix some things at their place and thought he should do it then. Meanwhile, Mary, Jesse, Sarah and little Maude settled in for the night.

When he returned, Mary was pleased to see his spirits were still good. They all sat and talked amicably as William whittled some wood chippings to start the morning's fire. Everything was quite normal. Around 9:00 p.m. they were asleep.

Sometimes between 10:00 p.m. and 11:00 p.m., the demon came out. A demon that would create a memory so horrific that all the praying in the world would never release it from your thoughts.

As it would be discovered, when William had taken the family to Romeo, his plan had been set. He had picked up a revolver and ten bullets at the hardware store. The gun and bullets he hid in the inside pocket of his coat.

Now, he pulled it out and carefully loaded each bullet into its chamber. The horror was about to begin.

Mary had awoken the moment William left the bed. She watched him go into the sitting room. He often got up and she initially didn't think much about it. Mary began to drift off when she heard him return. Through half-opened eyes, she saw something in his hand but didn't know what it was.

The next thing she recalled was an extremely bright flash in her face and a sudden, sharp pain just above the heart. For a moment it took her breath away.

She cried out, not immediately understanding what happened. Natural instincts, shock and pure adrenaline caused her to jump from the bed. He shot again, this time it struck her in the lower abdomen. She stumbled toward him and tried to struggle the gun away. That's when he brought out a hammer. He struck her head again and again. She managed to get the hammer away from William and threw it under the bed before collapsing to the floor in a semi-conscious state.

Their son, Jesse, had heard the gunshots and came running into the room. He saw his mother lying in a pool of blood and his father pacing the room with a revolver. Terrified, he immediately turned and ran back to his room, sliding under his bed, hiding as far back as he could.

Meanwhile, Sarah, hearing the shots, rushed into the room and stopped short at the horror before her. Without a word, her father turned and shot her. The bullet struck her side, tearing an ugly path to her groin. In paralyzing pain, she fell to the floor, immobile.

Little three-year old Maudie came out of her bedroom, sleepy-eyed and wondering what was happening. Without thought, William brought up the gun one more time and fired.

To his frustration, they were all still alive. With the hammer under his bed somewhere, he needed something better. He stopped briefly, thought for a few seconds and went to the woodshed. It was very dark in there. He couldn't find what he was looking for and began tossing things angrily around.

While he was outside Mary regained consciousness. She struggled to her knees and began crawling from the house. In her last effort and a mother's determination, she managed again to stand up. Clutching a hand to her chest, leaving a trail of blood behind her, she half-ran, half-staggered to the home of her brother, James Gulick. She pounded madly at the door and collapsed on the porch as they answered. Before losing complete consciousness, she cried out for them to save her family. William was murdering everyone.

Meanwhile, William returned from the shed. He now held a large wood axe and went to Sarah. Still laying prostrate on the floor, he raised the axe and brought it down on her head with a powerful whack. He raised it again, striking yet another horrible blow. Her body was still, her face unrecognizable.

He searched the house for Mary and couldn't find her. This only seemed to ignite a greater rage. Turning to little Maudie lying on the floor, he raised the axe and buried it in her head.

Throughout this, Jesse cowered under the fragile protection of his hiding place, his body trembling with fear. He watched from under the bed as his father approached him. His father began tearing apart his room, looking for him. Finally, his father's twisted, enraged face peered under the bed directly at him.

In a terrified whisper, Jesse asked, "Are you going to kill me, too, papa?"

Perhaps it was the sound of his son's voice that brought William back from whatever dark hell he had descended. He stared at Jesse for a moment and said, "No, don't be afraid, my boy. I won't kill you. Now listen. You will find $150 in my vest pocket when I am gone. I want you to get it and divide it with your sister, Phoebe."[1]

With that, William simply turned, dropped the bloodied axe on the floor, and left the house. Jesse ran from the opposite door to seek help from his father's family who lived down the street.

Between Mary's call and Jesse's, the Gulick and Williams family converged on the house. Neighbors also began showing up. None, however, wanted to go inside, fearing William was still on his murderous rampage. It was a nephew of William Major who, armed with a revolver and rifle, was brave enough to enter.

What he saw made the bile rise in his throat. Blood. Blood everywhere. Blood covering walls, ceiling, floors. Bed clothes thrown about, soaked with blood. Embedded with the blood were pieces of human flesh and hair.

William was nowhere to be seen but bodies were. He immediately saw the remains of Sarah, although her entire head was horribly mangled, making her almost unrecognizable. To his horror, the poor woman was still alive. Little Maudie was also still alive, although those who saw her condition couldn't understand how that was even possible. They sent for

---

1 "Murder and Suicide." *Saginaw Evening News.* 30 Dec. 1889: 1.

a doctor while those who remained did their best to stop the bleeding. Sadly, little Maudie passed within an hour of discovery. Sarah lasted more than a day but finally succumbed to her injuries.

So busy were they in tending to the victims, they didn't notice that it was now morning and no one had seen William. Some believed he likely ran off into the forest and killed himself. However, they would eventually find him hanging in his barn, an apparent suicide. He had died a slow death, his inexperience hampering the job and leading to a slow and painful asphyxiation. According to newspaper reports, the men who discovered his lifeless body left him in that condition for many hours.

Reports in newspapers said that Mary was still alive but so great was the extent of her injuries she would not live much longer. They underestimated Mary's determination. She did live. With a head bashed in and two bullets in her body, she lived, but her battle was long and filled with agony and crazed confusion. For several days she drifted in and out of consciousness, often rambling about things that didn't make sense. Mary would sometimes ask to see Jesse and told her caregivers she hoped they found William dead.

As she began to make more sense and her fever lessened, they interviewed her more extensively. Their main question, of course, was what had caused William's murderous act? Had there been a marital spat? Fighting? Mary told them no. There hadn't been any fights. In fact, she claimed he had been unusually kind and content in the days before.

The only possible reason might be land problems. Apparently William had talked to Sarah's husband, Joe, about coming to live on the farm and offered him 19 acres of land.

Initially, Joe said he might do that. So William turned over the deed for the property to Joe and started fixing up a small home that was there. However, Joe changed his mind after his brother asked him not to leave Ortonville.

That was a huge disappointment to William. He had a hard time letting go of the fact Joe didn't come. He was also upset when Joe did not immediately return the deed to him, leaving William with the thought he had been deceived and swindled by his son-in-law.

Yet, Mary didn't think that was the likely cause. Some felt she was holding something back, but she denied it.

There were rumors he also had money problems and decided to kill his family rather than find them destitute when he lost the farm. But that wasn't it either. After William's death, the house was scrubbed clean, and Mary continued to live in their Mt. Vernon home for many decades. As the years passed, William and Mary's son, Jesse, never married. He lived with his mother, working the farm.

They had enough money and the land produced enough income to keep it going for many years. So if money wasn't the cause for William's insane action, what was?

People said it was the very land on which the farm sat. It was evil. Contaminated. The woods surrounding the land was dark, dreary, and swampy. They said if a man walked through those woods, he would immediately be filled with gloom and think of bad things.

The townfolk said the evilness seemed to start back in 1874. It was then a little girl not far from the Major's place was caught sitting in those gloomy woods, playing with a Copperhead snake. The snake was very poisonous yet the child showed no concern as the Copperhead wrapped its body around her, gliding up her arms. The snake did not bite and, in fact, didn't even threaten the girl.

No one knew who the young girl was but all said she looked to be a very queer child. A few conjectured that the child wasn't a child at all but the very devil in disguise. Was it then the land became contaminated?

It was around that same time the Scarlet Fever epidemic came. Mt. Vernon seemed to be hit the worst. There were many deaths, mostly children.

Then began the suicides, too many for such a small area. There was the young woman who lived just over the hill from the Major farm. Her name was Ruth Rush. Like Major, she hanged herself in her home. Then came

Major's daughter, Pheobe, who would most certainly have killed herself if her mother hadn't found her in time. Next was the farm hand, not even a mile from the Major's place. For some unknown reason he also hanged himself. It was said there were others as well.

Researching this story, I came across a newspaper article on a family genealogy site. The name of the newspaper wasn't included but it did quote a neighbor of the Major family who was described as a big, pompous, intelligent-looking farmer. The man was certain the very land is what caused Major to become a maniac.

The farmer was quoted as saying, "Why I wouldn't give you five cents for all I can see from that hill. The whole neighborhood is haunted. It's a regular spook's paradise."[2]

Of course, can we seriously take the stories offered by the unnerved, superstitious townspeople in 1889 Mt. Vernon, Michigan? It's understandable to some degree. They needed to find a reason to explain why someone whom they knew fairly well would commit such a hideous act. It is very unlikely we'll ever know what caused William's mind to completely snap that December 28th evening.

I was curious about the area and what it looked like today. I found an old map comparing it to today's streets and identified the approximate location where the Major farm once stood. I made my way past the busy streets and drove through Utica, Shelby Township and Washington. I eventually turned off on a dirt road and quickly found myself in another time. The new homes, shops and perfectly paved streets were gone.

Here the roads were rough gravel and heavily wooded. The busy little community faded behind me as I slowly made my way down the trail. Not many homes were visible in this section of land. The few I could see were buried deep in the woods.

I finally arrived at what I believed was the location. There was a dirt road that had the semblance of a driveway. I couldn't initially see a home so I pulled my car off the road a bit and parked.

---

2 Woolever, Stewart J. A., Jr. "Biography of William R. Major, Warren, New Jersey." *USGen Web Archives - Census Wills Deeds Genealogy.* N.p., 2002. Web.

It was fairly remote. Even the sound of traffic was gone. The surrounding land was very natural and lush. Beautiful. Peaceful.

I moved up the dirt driveway a few dozen yards and saw a home that look fairly new sitting far back, hidden within the woods. Respectfully I backed away, wondering if the owners knew the history of the land on which their home sat. Wisely I decided it was best they didn't know.

I moved down the gravel road, away from the home into a section of land that was more wilderness. It was thick with trees, wild shrubbery, and tall weeds. There was a section of land that seemed to be slightly raised. I carefully moved through the overgrowth, checking the ground for possible signs of an old foundation.

I couldn't be sure because of the thick weeds and the packed-down layers of dead leaves long discarded by their trees over decades of falls past. However, I did come to a section of land that appeared to contain a portion of some foundation. It could have been the foundations of an old storage shed. Of course, my mind went to the thought that it could possibly be the remains of the Major farmhouse.

It was so quiet and peaceful in this area long gone to wilderness. I tried to imagine how different it must have been that winter night over 130 years ago.

Something caught my eye within the weeds. I walked over and to my amazement I found just one flower growing in amongst the trees and wild growth. A single flower amongst the weeds. I left feeling overwhelmed.

The Fate of
Sister Mary Janina

Isadore/Cedar, MI

A small town in the Leelanau Peninsula nestled between the rolling hills and lush woodlands of the Sleeping Bear Sand Dunes and Traverse City holds the secret to one of Michigan's most controversial mysteries. A mystery that merges a cover-up, scandal and murder with a curse and a lost soul on a solitary journey.

What happened to Sister Mary Janina, a young Roman Catholic Felician nun of the St. Isadore Convent who went missing in late August 1907? The answer and her fate is sealed somewhere in a small box in an unmarked Michigan grave.

Let's push open a forbidden door that leads to a dark, endless room. Put on your detective hat. I can't solve this mystery, but perhaps you can. Let's start at the beginning.

According to the most consistent ancestry records, Jan and Josefa Mezek immigrated to America from Bohemia (Czech Republic) June 17, 1867. With them came their children, Mary, Anna, Elizabeth and Joseph.

Hearing that employment was plentiful in Illinois for any able-bodied man not afraid of work, John moved his family to Chicago. There they shared a small residence on

Photo opposite: Nineteenth-century slums of Chicago, once home to Sister Mary Janina. (Chicago History Museum, CHi-021975)

111

Fisk Street with several other immigrant families. Space was definitely limited at the small home, but that wasn't unusual for newly immigrated folks trying to get started in a new country.

Within a year, their oldest daughters, Mary, Anna and Lizzie, married and moved away as the Mezek family continued to grow. Their next son, Frank, was born and a few years later, around February 1873, little Josephine arrived. It was in 1875 the first tragedy struck the family. Mrs. Mezek gave birth to twins, a boy and girl. The boy was named Emmanuel and the girl, Emilia. Sadly, death took the little girl at some point between 1875 and 1880.

Holy Rosary Church in 1909 (Traverse City Area Historical Society)

It was during that same period the family moved to a home at 111 Bunker Street, an area known to be in the heart of one of Chicago's worst slum areas. The Mezeks shared the residence with 18 other people.

Keeping their small space clean was a challenge for Josephine. With poor plumbing and only one toilet amongst the 18 residents, sanitation was a serious problem.

What the family may not have known at the time is that Bunker Street carried a dark reputation. It was said a fearful entity or Dybbuk roamed the street and got into residents who were sinners and not true God-fearing people.

In 1939, an interview was conducted of former resident, Hilda Polacheck. She had lived on Bunker Street as a young child and recalled the story of the Dybbuk. She described the conditions she lived in:

"I remember that house on Bunker Street where the dybbuk was supposed to go from place to place. That house was built for one family but when we live there, six families were living in the house. No one had a bathroom. There was one toilet in the hall for the six families and some of them had as many as six or eight kids."[1]

Hilda recalled how her father had been brought home early from work one day. He looked very sick. Her mother went for a doctor as the little girl was sent outside.

As she waited on the home's front stoop, she heard the women talking. They said Dybbuk had gotten into her father. They thought he must have done something wrong for this to have happened, but little Hilda could not imagine what that could have been. Her father worked all day and ate home every night. He didn't have time to do anything wrong.

Two days later he died and her mother had to go to work making much less than her father. Times became very hard. Her mother no longer got out the old washtub to bathe Hilda and the little girl's clothes were no longer clean. She was only given a penny for a roll at lunch. Her mother had also become mean, taking to crying or scolding little Hilda every night. Hilda thought Dybbuk had gotten into her as well.

The truth was that bad things did happened to residents on Bunker Street. There were frequent accounts of serious illness. Typhoid and other diseases swept through the neighborhood, killing many. There was also a high incidence of violence and murder.

The cause for this was more likely the hard life of surviving in the slums and poor sanitation than the Dybbuk. However, on Bunker Street many still believed it was the Dybbuk that caused these conditions to exist and cursed the residents.

Dybbuk or not, the lives of the Mezek family continued. Certainly it was not an easy life, but they remained strong through their love of each other and their abiding faith in God. Like many Polish and Bohemian families, they were devout Roman Catholics.

---

1 Polacheck, Hilda. [The Dybbuk of Bunker Street]. Chicago, Illinois, 1939. Manuscript/Mixed Material. Retrieved from the Library of Congress, <https://www.loc.gov/item/wpalh000080/>.

The Mezeks were members of Chicago's St. Francis Bohemian Roman Catholic Society and participated in many of the church events. In early January 1883, the Society held a fair followed by a dance. It was a joyful social event and a needed break from the drudgery of life. As unlikely as it may have seemed earlier in the day, the lives of the Mezek family were about to be forever, irrevocably changed.

That evening the music started and people began to dance. The hall was filled with laughter, loud voices and happy people.

John's son, Joseph, was the family's hot head, a scrapper. He was a good son who loved his family but Joseph had a very difficult time controlling his anger. As liquor flowed, Joseph's temper flared and a fight began. Joseph was on the losing end of the fight. John stepped in to help his son when a police officer, Peter Soergl, arrived.

Apparently John, his own temper kicking up, got into an argument with Officer Soergi over his son's involvement in the fight. It wasn't a physical argument nor did John threaten the officer. It was more of a verbal disagreement.

Officer Sosergi did something he had never done before. Without provocation, he suddenly pulled his revolver and shot John Mezek, point blank. John dropped to the floor in front of the officer, dead.

The room instantly grew silent. They couldn't believe what had just happened. John Mezek was a fine, upstanding man. He had never caused problems. In fact, he had never violated the law. Now his life had instantly been swept away. What had just happened?

Shouts of anger rose as Officer Soergl backed away and left. Within a few days the St. Francis Bohemian Roman Catholic Society filed a complaint. Soergl was arrested, tried and found guilty of manslaughter. He was sentenced to the state prison with a sentence of one to fourteen years.

While justice had been done in the criminal action, there was no justice for John's widow or family. Josephine was without her man and the children without a father.

Shock and grief from the sudden, violent death of her husband was more than Josephine could take. She went into a deep depression, removed herself from life and slowly lost her mind. Three months later, a court found her insane and she was committed to the Illinois Eastern Hospital for the Insane. There she would remain until her death.

Something had to be done with the Mezek children. The two oldest boys, Joseph and Frank, had jobs and were old enough to take care of themselves. The youngest, Emil, was sent to another family. Finally, it was

Detroit Felician House orphans, 1883. Somewhere in this group of children is Josephine Mezek. (Steven Keller, Historian)

decided that little Josephine would be sent to a Polish convent of Felician sisters in the Detroit area.

In a matter of a few short weeks, the children's lives had been torn apart. Grieving their father's violent death and the sudden, traumatizing mental disease of their mother, they were left with nothing to hold on to but each other. Now, even that was about to end.

We can only imagine the turmoil and fear little Josephine was going through during this time. She had to leave all she'd ever known and travel to a place far from home to live with complete strangers.

Days turned into weeks, weeks into months and months faded to years. Young Josephine grew up in the cloistered protection of the Felician nuns. She was unknowing of worldly ways. Her life with the nuns was all she ever knew. Between the age of 14-15 she decided to join her Holy Sisters and began the slow process of becoming a nun.

It was a few weeks before Christmas, 1900, when she received the horrible news. Her brother, Joseph, had committed suicide. Apparently he had been abusive to his wife. Fearing for her life, his wife ran to her brother's house for protection. The brother and Joseph got into an argument and Joseph shot him, three times, at close range. A miracle had happened; the brother-in-law's injuries were not life threatening. However, after shoot-

Sister Mary Janina (Used with permission: The World Wide Magazine)

ing his brother-in-law, Joseph placed the gun to his head and ended his life.

Sister Janina's thoughts at the moment are unknown. Most certainly she was in shock knowing her brother was dead, his final actions horrific and, in the eyes of God and the Church, a mortal sin. It would mean the eternal damnation of his soul. She prayed to God for His forgiveness of Joseph's actions and that He would have mercy on her brother's soul and save him from the eternal fires of Hell.

August 25, 1901, Josephine Mezek joined her Godly sisters and took final vows of the Felician Order. They placed an iron and steel ring on the third finger of her left hand symbolizing her faith and commitment to Jesus and the Church and a sacred promise of chastity, poverty, charity, and obedience. Engraved on the ring were Polish words that translated to Jesus my all, Detroit, 1901. Josephine Mezek then left her past and worldly name behind and became Sister Mary Janina.

Sister Mary Janina was described as a slender, petite woman standing just over five feet. She had dark red hair that was cropped short as she entered the sisterhood. Although not considered beautiful in the traditional sense, she was attractive in a gentle, pleasant way.

Janina was an outgoing, personable young woman, considered quite intelligent but not always the best pupil. Truth be told, she sometimes did not precisely follow the rules. There was a compelling, irresistible way about her that made her well liked by her superiors although not always her peers.

She was also musically gifted with a beautiful voice and was a skilled pianist. Sister Janina loved playing and singing, often losing herself in the melody and words of the hymns. Her favorite hymn was *Jesus, Lover of My Soul.*

Although not the best student, she did become a teacher and excelled at it. She loved children and was said to be patient, kind and loving towards them, although some thought her teaching methods a little too liberal. In spite of that or because of it, her students performed very well under her instruction.

One day a cough started. At first it was merely a nagging thing. She thought it may have been an allergy or a slight cold that would clear up. In time, the cough grew worse and the doctor's diagnosis came. Somewhere she had contracted tuberculosis. It was now active. With so many tragedies and tribulations in her life, could she fight through yet another? She put her faith in God and trusted He would guide her in the right direction.

At the time it was thought the best treatment for the disease was fresh, open air. Mother Superior contemplated what to do with poor Sister Mary Janina.

There was a small church in the northwestern section of Lower Michigan called Holy Rosary Roman Catholic Church located in Isadore, a small community in the Leelanau area. Its residents were primarily Polish immigrants with devout Roman Catholic faith.

It was a beautiful area of the state with lush trees and rolling hills. The little church was even set on top of a hill with plenty of cool, clean, fresh air.

There was, however, one eerie landscape that flawed this otherwise beautiful location. It was an extremely dense swamp behind the church and convent. Tall spruce, tamarack and cedars covered this area, which was a swamp filled with dangerous undergrowth and deep bog-holes. It was a location where people could get lost if they didn't know where they were going. The inexperienced did not stray into the swamp alone.

On a whole, however, the location could not be more ideal for someone in Sister Janina's condition. In fact, two other nuns at Holy Rosary were also afflicted with tuberculosis.

So it was, in 1906, around the age of 33, Sister Mary Janina was re-assigned as head teacher and Mother Superior of Holy Rosary Church. That is where she met Father Andrew Bieniawski and his housekeeper, Stanislawa (Stella) Lipczynska.

Andrew Bieniawski was born in November 1874. He was raised in Poland but of Russian decent. He immigrated to the United States around 1897 and was ordained the same year. Several years later he was assigned as pastor of Holy Rosary Church.

Father Bieniawski stood nearly 6 feet tall with brown eyes and dark, thick hair. It was said he looked quite dashing in his black cassock.

He was devout in his religious beliefs and a priest with great ambition. Although he was a man of few words, when engaged in conversation he did display a keen sense of wit. Most of his time was spent on Church business; however, he did take time to enjoy his two favorite pastimes, fishing and beekeeping. He also had a fascination with animals, including some exotic creatures like alligators, massive snakes, foxes, etc. He kept them in the back of the rectory and called them his menagerie.

Living with Father Bieniawski was his younger sister, Susan; his housekeeper, Mrs. Stella Lipczynska; and her daughter, Mary. Stella was a widow about 38 years of age and of diminutive size, standing well under five feet. She managed not only the rectory but also prepared meals, maintained the garden and managed the priest's animal menagerie. After her husband's death, her faith grew even stronger. Her life now centered around God, the Church, her daughter, and Father Bieniawski.

Although Sister Janina and Father Bieniawski never openly shared their impression of one another, they did seem to get along very well. As the months passed, Father would often visit Sister Janina's classroom. After school, he would seek out her company and the two would frequently be seen talking or laughing together.

Stella did not like this one bit. She told the Father it was inappropriate to spend so much time with Sister Janina. People were talking. She suggested the Father stay away from the young nun. It was wrong!

Indeed, gossip was spreading that the priest and nun had become romantically involved. There was one student, living at the rectory for a time, who claimed he saw the priest come up behind Sister Janina while she was playing the piano. According to the student, the priest placed his hands over her eyes and kissed her.

It was the end of the school year, 1907, and things were looking up for Sister Janina. Though still somewhat weak from her tuberculosis, her coughing and breathing had improved since her arrival at Holy Rosary.

The nuns at the northern Michigan convent usually returned to Detroit after school was over. This year, however, Sister Janina and the two other sisters with tuberculosis received permission to remain. They were very happy. Not only was the fresh air good for their health but they loved the beautiful area. It was, without question, much prettier than the highly populated, urban community of Detroit.

The summer of 1907 was especially busy. The new brick school had just been completed. It was quite beautiful. The previous wooden school had burned down under suspicious curcumstances. Who may have set the fire was unknown. The new school was built of brick specifically to make it much less likely to be destroyed in a similar way.

To celebrate the new school, Bishop Richter was planning to give a dedication ceremony on August 24th. Sister Janina was in charge of arranging the entertainment and church decorations and found herself extremely busy making wax and paper flowers for the church and embroidered cloths for the altars. Most of the materials for these decorations were kept in the church basement.

Packages with materials for the decorations were being delivered to the church on a regular basis. One day, however, an unusual package came from Sears and Roebucks. It contained civilian clothes. At first, they wondered why the sister would want to purchase civilian clothes, but the priest thought she had likely bought them for a needy person in the church. It would be something she would do. Nothing more was thought about it at the time.

On August 22 and 23, wanting a break before Bishop Richter came, Father Bieniawski decided to go fishing. On the 22nd he went to Lime Lake with Jacob Flees, the parish's sexton. On the 23rd he went to Carp Lake with Theodore Gruba, a parish helper and choirboy, and the Father's sister, Susan. It was during his absence on the afternoon of August 23 that Sister Mary Janina went missing.

The day had passed much like other days. Nothing unusual. The two nuns had taken their usual mid-day nap. During this time, Sister Janina would retreat to the front room to read her prayer book. When the nuns awoke later that afternoon, Sister Janina was gone.

In their search for her, they found her prayer book lying open on a window sill. This was very unusual. Sister Janina kept her prayer book in a small pocket in the shoulder of her brown robe at all times. She wouldn't just leave it out like that. Another disturbing revelation was the discovery of her large rosary, which was normally attached to her waist cord, hanging from the doorknob of her room.

The sisters had also found the door to the first floor workroom had been unlocked and left open, exposing the swamp behind the convent. That door was never left open while the nuns were sleeping.

As their search continued, they would find that Sister Janina or someone had entered the rear of the church and gone into the basement, perhaps to get materials for making flowers. They entered the basement but no one was there.

At first the nuns were not immediately alarmed, believing Sister Janina may have been a little careless with her prayer book and rosary. The open door on the first floor of the convent made them think she had gone for a walk. However, when early evening came and she had not returned, the nuns became very worried. They went to the parish house to ask the housekeeper, Stella, if she'd seen her.

When they entered the rectory, Stella was busy in the kitchen making loaves of bread and cakes for the Bishop's arrival. They asked if she'd seen Sister Janina. She told them she had not and continued her baking. Stella's daughter, Mary, also claimed not to have seen Janina. That's when the nuns knew something was very wrong.

Father Bieniawski and his fishing partners arrived later that night. He had barely arrived when Stella, along with Sisters Josephina and Mary, came rushing to him. The nuns would later recount that, previous to the priest's return, Stella had seemed unconcerned about Sister Janina. However, her demeanor quickly changed when the priest returned.

Bieniawski was in disbelief. Sister Janina missing? When did it happen? Why?

After the nuns explained, the priest ordered everyone search through the buildings and grounds again. When nothing new was found, he told the sisters to discreetly call upon some of the neighbors. He didn't want to worry them or stir up gossip but wanted to know if anyone had seen her. That, too, was futile.

By the end of the evening, everyone was exhausted and worried. Nothing more could be done until morning and they lay down for what would be a restless night.

At some point in the late evening or early morning hours, the nuns awoke to the sound of a horse-driven rig moving past the convent. The noise from the rig was very distinguishable, the familiar sound bouncing clearly through the quiet night air.

The next day the nuns spoke of the passing carriage. They also said that Sister Janina had seemed to be unusually quiet and sad in the days prior to her disappearance. Perhaps she had been rethinking her life in the Church and had made a decision to leave her vows behind. That may be the reason for her purchasing the civilian clothes. Father Bieniawski believed this highly improbable but he could not entirely dismiss the idea.

The Leelanau County Sheriff, Martin Brown, was contacted. Yet another search was made with the same empty results. A more thorough interview was done with the neighbors. No one had seen her.

Then gossip began. It was said a local doctor, George Fralick, had been making frequent, private visits to Sister Janina's room. The visits occurred once a week, sometimes more. Although the doctor's visit was needed for evaluation of Janina's tuberculosis, once a week seemed excessive. It was forbidden that a man, any man, enter a nun's room without another nun being present. This protocol was followed during Dr. Fralick's earlier visits but lately he visited her room alone.

Gossip also said Father Bieniawski had been seen entering Sister Janina's room alone. This reinforced the belief of some that there was a romantic relationship with one or both men. Had the nun been pregnant? Was that another possible reason for Dr. Fralick's frequent visits?

If she were pregnant, that would account for her disappearance. To avoid the humiliation and shame, she would have left town to have the baby. The civilian clothes she had purchased were to be worn to hide her status as a Felician nun.

The Bishop arrived for the scheduled school dedication that Sunday but the ceremony was postponed. Instead, after Sunday services, Father Bieniawski announced the disappearance of Sister Janina and asked for everyone's help in finding her.

While Sheriff Brown began organizing search parties, Father Bieniawski was on another mission to find Sister Janina. He traveled to Detroit to talk to the Mother House to see if they'd heard from her. Then, with his own money, he hired a highly reputable Detroit detective named Castle to conduct a separate search.

There was a sheriff in Bellaire who had a bloodhound that had been used to successfully track down several lost people in the Upper Peninsula. His name was Bill Kittle and his trusted bloodhound was Tom. Again, with his own money, Father Bieniawski hired Sheriff Kittle and Tom.

Unfortunately, when they arrived at the convent the nuns had freshly washed all of the Sister's clothing and the hound was unable to pick up a scent. In a last ditch effort, they used Janina's prayer book left on the windowsill and rosary left hanging on the doorknob.

Tom picked up just enough of a scent to respond. With a rolling howl, the dog led them through the convent door. They followed the dog through a cornfield, skirted the swamp, and across a public highway. While searching, they came across a barbed wired fence and saw a piece of brown wool

Map showing the church, convent, and trail the bloodhound first took but quickly lost the scent. (Used with permission: The World Wide Magazine)

cloth. It was similar to the wool robes the Felician nuns wore. Maybe they were getting somewhere!

Unfortunately, not long after, Tom stopped, uncertain. He circled a few times but whatever trail he had been following was gone.

On their return, Sheriff Kittle showed the brown cloth to the priest, who showed it to the nuns. They agreed the material was similar to a Felician nun's robe.

As they continued their conversation, Kittle mentioned something he'd heard that caught his attention. At one point, while the dog was on-scent, Kittle could have sworn he heard a woman's voice coming from somewhere in the swamp. It could have been his imagination, of course.

123

However, it seemed possible Sister Janina may have gone into the swamp and gotten lost. They needed to re-focus their search on the swamp.

That evening something interesting occurred. An aged woman who lived near the wooded marsh reported a strange incident at her home. She had been awakened by the sound of singing. It was a woman's voice singing a hymn.

She looked out the window, stared into the thick cedars and was surprised to see the light of what might be a candle slowly moving through the woods. She wasn't sure if it was a candle, however, because the light didn't flicker like a normal candle.

The old woman continued to see the light and hear the singing. Finally, after five minutes or so, the light disappeared and so did the singing. It was the strangest thing.

The next day the two remaining nuns at St. Isadore Convent left. They had become very distraught over the disappearance of Sister Janina. Their eating habits had greatly diminished. When asked to stay they refused, indicating they were fearful that whatever happened to Sister Mary Janina may happen to them. There was nothing that could keep them there.

That evening Sheriff Kittle set up a base camp at Holy Rosary. There would be a 24-hour surveillance. Men were stationed on the roads and would hold watch in rotations throughout the night.

As night fell, the Sheriff, along with a couple of newspaper reporters and a few members of the watch team, settled in to sleep. It was around 2:00 a.m. when they were awakened by a sound. They looked outside. There was a waning moon that night, casting faint light across the area. Yet, through the darkness, they saw a shadowy figure moving away from the convent into the swamp. It was too dark to track and they decided to wait until morning.

As the sun rose, Sheriff Kittle, Tom, and a small search team headed off. They quickly found fresh prints. The footprints were small and, Kittle thought, like that of a woman.

His dog, Tom, picked up a scent and with the familiar howl he pushed against his restraints as he headed into the swamp. The woods grew dense. Progress was slow. As the pine trees closed in around the men and ground grew more wet, Tom lost the trail. Failure again.

It was September 1, about nine days after Janina went missing, Father Bieniawski gave an early morning mass pleading once again for the community to come together. They responded and more than 400 people converged around the church.

Led by sheriffs from area communities, the men spread out about 20 feet apart. Like a living wall, the group swept into the dense swamp. It was very difficult going in many places but they were determined and pushed through the harsh brush, extremely dense thickets, tangled barbs, fallen logs and deep bogs. They meticulously inspected everything in their path, taking their time, searching for a body, a trail or anything that might offer a clue to the fate of Sister Mary Janina.

The hunt continued until more than five solid miles had been covered. The more they searched, the more confusing things became.

Footprints were found miles into the swamp in places where no sane person would wander. The prints were old, at least a week maybe more. As before, the prints just appeared out of nowhere and ended just as abruptly as they started. This made no sense to Sheriff Kittle who took great pride in his experience as a tracker.

They eventually came to a small, clear brook and were encouraged to discover a small indentation by the smooth bank. It suggested someone small, perhaps Sister Janina, had knelt to drink fresh water. Unfortunately the trail went cold and, as before, nothing further was found.

Another day grew into evening and they settled down for the night. A couple of teams remained in the swamp. It was very late in the evening when one team saw what they thought was candlelight, again moving through the cedars. They also heard the singing. They called out Janina's name and moved in that direction. Fearing they might get lost in the darkness, they didn't go too far. Whoever it was out there did not respond to their calls and quickly disappeared in the darkness.

The next day, guards were stationed around the parameters of the swamp with timed rotations to make sure the entire swamp area was guarded throughout the night. No one would get in or out without being seen.

The guards silently held their vigil with nothing but the familiar sounds of crickets, toads, and cicadas filling their ears. No one traveled the roads. Other than the natural swamp sounds, things were extremely quiet.

It was in the late hours of the night when it began. One of the guards suddenly stood, his eyes intent, trying to see into the inky blackness of the dense pine forest. He thought he'd heard something. A guard near him motioned. He'd heard it as well. Singing.

The voice sounded like a woman's but wasn't normal. They claimed there was an eerie tone. To their ears it didn't sound like the voice of a living woman. The singing was coming from deep within the swamp. How had this woman entered without their seeing or had she never left the swamp? Had she found a hiding place undiscovered during their previous search?

They weren't the only men on watch that night that heard the singing. Others had as well. It was a hymn. A familiar melody. Father Bieniawski knew the hymn. The Sheriff and members of the watch team knew the hymn. It was Sister Janina's favorite, *Jesus, Lover of My Soul*.

The guards did not move to investigate. Neither did the sheriff. No one did. Fear was the anchor that held them in place. Who was that? What was that?

The next morning, word quickly spread. If that was Sister Janina wandering the woods, lost, she must have gone insane just like her mother.

There were a few in town, folks more prone to superstitious beliefs, who whispered *Wila*. According to Slavic supernatural belief, a Wila is the spirit of a once living woman who had lived a frivolous or wicked life. Because of that, her spirit floats between this earth and the afterlife. Wilas are said to have beautiful voices. Though generally not harmful, they are capable of killing someone who defies them.

Wilas seek refuge in the wilderness. The swamp would be an ideal place for a Wila. If Sister Janina had a romantic relationship with the priest or doctor, that would be more than frivolous. It would be a mortal sin. Could Sister Janina be dead and her hopeless soul wandering in a limbo somewhere between earth and heaven? Had she become a Wila?

Eleven days into the search and authorities, approaching this frustrating case from an objective perspective, came to the conclusion that Sister Mary Janina was still alive and perhaps within a few miles of Isadore. Frustrated by their lack of progress and looking for any avenues that may provide a clue or direction, they accepted the offer of two clairvoyants who claimed they could help.

One clairvoyant's trance offered nothing specific. The other claimed to see the nun being hidden in the basement of a square house somewhere around Glen Lake. Based on the clairvoyant's description of the home, the sheriff and members of the church searched the homes around Glen Lake. Like other possible leads, it went nowhere. More frustration.

On September 8, 1907 Bishop Richter finally gave the school's dedication. The program for the event and decorations seen throughout the church were made by the hands of Sister Janina. During the dedication, Father Bieniawski pleaded to his parishioners not to give up the search for Sister Janina and offered a $500 reward for anyone who found her alive or dead.

The reward money brought out throngs of people, from inexperienced thrill-seekers and wanna-be detectives to serious investigators. Even then, with all these people and various search parties, nothing turned up.

This confusing, complex, strange story is about to get even stranger. A few days after Bishop Richter's dedication, September 12, an anonymous letter arrived from Chicago addressed to the Mother Superior of St. Isodore Convent.

The letter stated that Sister Mary Janina was neither killed nor abducted. She had just gotten tired of the job and went away. The letter asked the authorities to give up their search and their belief she had been abducted. No matter how much they searched, they would not find her and, in fact, she didn't want them to find her. The letter was signed Protestant Pup.

Father Bieniawski looked at the handwritten letter and noted a certain familiarity to the script. It bore similarities to Dr. Fralick's writing. The priest began to seriously consider Dr. Fralick's involvement in Sister Janina's disappearance.

Sheriff Brown came up with another possibility. Since the letter was postmarked from Chicago and Janina's family lived in Chicago, could it have come from them? He wrote to them about the letter. They quickly responded saying it had not come from them nor had they known of their sister's whereabouts. They redirected the responsibility back to the church to find out what happened to their sister.

Adding to Father Bieniawski's frustration, even the detective he had hired gave up. In all the years he had worked in the field, Detective Castle claimed he had never worked on anything quite so difficult.

Eventually the case went cold and the newspapers lost interest in the story. One final thing was about to happen, however. Just one more curious piece to an unidentifiable puzzle was about to be added.

Two months later, St. Isadore's new Mother Superior went into the basement of the church to get some decorations for the upcoming holiday. No one had been in the basement since the search teams had left several months before.

While down there she saw something on the dirt floor that caught her attention. It was a pair of steel-rimmed glasses. The syle was similar to those worn by Felician nuns. The Mother Superior knew Sister Janina and had seen her wearing such glasses.

She took her find to Father Bieniawski, who was immediately surprised. How did they get there? When?

During the weeks and months that followed Sister Janina's disappearance, on many occasions people had searched every inch of the basement. How was it possible a pair of glasses sitting on top of the dirt could have been overlooked? No glasses were reported missing by any of the convent's nuns.

To his knowledge, no one had recently entered the basement. If they weren't Janina's glasses, whose glasses were they? Had someone purposefully placed them in the basement? Like all the other clues in this case, the discovery did not help bring anyone closer to discovering the fate of Sister Mary Janina.

Christmas passed and the new year came. The case of the missing sister faded. It was generally accepted that Sister Janina had either been abducted by some unknown party or run away from the church and her vows and would never be seen again.

Fast forward eleven years. Father Bieniawksi was no longer pastor of Holy Rosary. The Church sent him away when the parishioners grew angry and distrustful of the priest, blaming him for the disappearance of Sister Janina.

Stella had gone to live with her now-married daughter in Wisconsin where she would remain for a short time. She would eventually return to

Father Bieniawski and his church in Manistee when the priest's sister became ill.

Replacing Father Bieniawski was Father Leopold Oprychalski. Father Leo quickly settled in his role as pastor and

Holy Rosary Church today (Roger Popa)

parishioners loved him. Then, to their great surprise and disappointment, Father Leo unexpectedly left. The townspeople wondered at his sudden departure.

In May of 1918, Father Edward Podleweski became the new pastor. Podleweski was young, short in stature with a very slender frame. He hired Martha Miller, a girl of about 18, to take care of the church. Apparently,

Martha Miller also took care of Father Podleweski. An indiscretion was made and the girl became pregnant. Podleweski was the biological father.

She promised the priest not to tell her parents he was the father. In turn, Father Podlaszewski promised to help her through the pregnancy. He drove her to St. Joseph's Sister of Mercy Hospital in Ann Arbor, a very reputable Catholic hospital that served as a safe haven for unmarried pregnant women.

After the baby was born and given up for adoption, Father Podleweski drove Martha back home. She was rather forlorn during that ride and, for some reason, Father Podleweski decided to confide one of his deepest held secrets. He and the church sexton, Jacob Flees, had just removed the remains of Sister Mary Janina from the floor of the church's basement and secretly buried her in the Holy Rosary cemetery.

He went on to explain that he'd first heard of the nun's remains being buried in the church's basement from Sister Leoncia, of the Detroit Felician Order, in 1917. At the time, he didn't believe the story.

However, when it was known a new brick church would be built over the foundations of the original church, his predecessor, Father Leo, contacted him. He recommended Podleweski remove the body of Sister Janina from the basement of the church before construction began. The church would want to avoid the scandalous publicity something like this would elicit. How had Father Leo learned of this?

The last and most important warning came from the Chaplain of the Felician order, Father Lempka. The chaplain told Podleweski the young nun had been killed and buried under the basement floor and her remains would be found under a pile of boards. He requested Podleweski remove the sister's remains before construction began.

How had the chaplain heard of this? It was whispered that it had come from a bishop in Wisconsin named Edward Kozlowski.

It was not something Father Podleweski or Flees took lightly. In fact, it was dreadful and one of the worst, most horrifying and shameful things they had done in their lives.

The height of the basement was oddly shaped. It was high enough to stand up at the back but short in the front, causing them to stoop. Flees started the job using a single lantern to light the area. He removed a section of stacked wooden boards and, using a spade, began to feel for a soft spot in the dirt. It took him a couple of times but he found it. Digging his spade into one soft area, he hit something. It turned out to be a bone.

Together Flees and Podleweski began the onerous, awful task of removing the bones. Flees would carefully expose one bone after another using a farmer's potato masher (a tool similar to a pitchfork but with shorter, broader tines.) Podlaszewski took them and placed them in a wooden box he had found. With the bones came large clumps of brown wool fabric with the color and thickness of a Felecian nun's robe. They uncovered sections of the waist cord used to cinch in the robe and a portion of the dark material from a Felician nun's veil.

The burial site itself wasn't deep, perhaps 18 inches. It was also not long. The body had been bent. Knees were up and pressed to the chest and the head bowed forward. When they thought all the remains had been collected, they brought up the box.

The next day, nuns at the convent were shown the bits of girdle and cloth and they confirmed they were portions of a Felician nun's habit. Later that day, Flees built a two-foot wooden box and carefully moved the remains and shreds of garments into the new box. In the dark of night, he buried it in the Holy Rosary Cemetery. It was near the large crucifix still standing today in the cemetery's yard. To obscure the freshly turned soil, he planted shrubs and a rosebush over the area.

Several months later, the Mother Superior from Detroit phoned the priest to ask if he had buried Sister Janina's remains in the cemetery. He confirmed he had. She was satisfied that Sister Janina had been interred in consecrated grounds. With the terrible tragedy of her life and death, it was the very least the Catholic Church could do for her.

After Father Podlewski finished telling the entire story, Martha sat in disbelief, shocked that something as horrible as this had happened. She promised she would not reveal this terrible secret. As it would turn out, she did not keep that promise. When her parents pressured her about the baby and its father, she revealed the priest. She also told them the secret of Sister Janina.

Scenes and Figures in Nun Mystery Case at Leland

Images from the trial: Top Right - Stanislawa (Stella) Lipczynska; Bottom Right - Father Andrew Bieniawski; Top Left - Leland Courthouse; Bottom Left - Jurors. (Traverse City Record, courtesy Traverse City District Library)

Her parents immediately went to the sheriff with the news. Within a short time, word spread throughout the county. The probate judge of Leelanau County had been the sheriff at the time of Janina's disappearance. He and the current sheriff got Jacob Flees to point out the area he had buried the remains. Soon after, the authorities took possession.

Forensic methods used today were, of course, non-existent in 1918. As a result, there was no way authorities could confirm if the remains were those of Sister Janina. They were also unable to determine the cause of death. Although, since the skull was fractured, it was thought it might have been a blow to the head. There was also no way for them to determine if the female had been pregnant.

The sheriff and his team went back to the church's basement and carefully sifted through the sand where the body had once been. Through this slow, tedious process they uncovered smaller bones and some very important artifacts. Were the smaller bones that of a fetus or simply the smaller bones of an adult skeleton? Details were not clear. Artifacts included a nun's scapular and a very unusual thimble with a unique design.

Also found was a crucifix, a spool of red thread that was wrapped in the remnants of a Traverse City newspaper which just happened to have a date near the time Sister Janina went missing. They also uncovered an iron and silver ring with an inscription on the inside that included the location and date of Sister Janina's final vows. Only 22 nuns in Detroit were given the ring on August 25, 1901. The ring and thimble, which was identified as Sister Janina's, led authorities to believe the remains were that of Sister Mary Janina.

The coroner's examination said the fracture on the left temporal area of the skull was the likely cause of death. It was severe enough to have created a hemorrhage. Although the hemorrhage would not cause immediate death, it would have led to eventual death. With that, a homicide was identified. Upon a further search of the basement, they came up with an old farmer's potato-masher that may have been used as the weapon, although no blood was discovered on the tool.

Immediate suspicion fell on Father Bieniawski and his housekeeper, Stella Lipczynska. The motive for Father Bieniawski was an unwanted romantic entanglement with Sister Janina and the possibility of pregnancy. For Stella Lipczynska, it was her dislike of the nun and her anger and jealousy over the closeness Father Bieniawski had with the sister.

Once they discovered Andrew Bieniawski had a clean alibi, they quickly turned their attention to his housekeeper, Stella. They had been told Stella had spoken ill words of Sister Janina and there were those who claimed the housekeeper had physically assaulted Janina on more than one occasion.

The nuns at the convent were afraid of the housekeeper's violent temperament. In fact, after Janina's disappearance, the nuns became fearful of even eating the food, beliving Stella may have poisoned it.

In February 1918, Judge Brown and Leelanau County Sherriff Kinnucan obtained an arrest warrant for Stella at St. Joseph's Church in Manistee where she continued to serve as housekeeper for Father Bieniawski. There she was taken into custody.

Although living in the U.S. for many years, Stella knew very little English and an interpreter had to be brought in to conduct the interrogations. Bail was set at $4,500. This was a huge amount of money in those days, a sum that would equate to over $100,000 today. Father Bieniawski was very adamant that Stella not spend a single night in jail. He immediately made arrangements with a bail bondsman and Stella was, at least temporarily, free.

A month later, in March, the housekeeper was given a hearing in Leland. This time she was sent to jail without bail where she would await trial.

Preparing for the trial was complex and difficult. Unfortunately, the two nuns who had last seen Sister Janina alive were unavailable. One was quite ill and the other had passed away. Also unfortunate, Bishop Edward Kozlowsi, the man who had first passed on knowledge of Sister Janina's murder, had died.

Wanting to build a stronger prosecution, a private undercover detective, Mary Tylicki, was hired. They trumped up an erroneous arrest charge and placed her in Stella's cell. Her goal was to gain the housekeeper's trust and get a confession. Mary would stay with Stella for the next few days. Stella and Mary were sometimes seen whispering together. The prosecutors hoped their tactic was working and Stella was sharing her dark secret with the detective.

As the days progressed, the housekeeper began acting stranger and stranger. She would sit silently, unresponsive. Her arm would extend in a position that looked as if she were playing an unseen violin and would hold that pose for some time. She was also seen rolling on the floor and talking gibberish. She would not eat. Her attorneys attempted to see her but were refused admittance into her cell.

Stella's actions eventually became so deranged they sent her to the psychiatric ward at the University of Michigan for observation. The doctors there studied her strange behavior for a month and asked for a time extension for further observation.

During that period, the housekeeper told the doctors that people at the jail were treating her cruelly. They tortured her. One time, as she explained, they took her to a dark room with only candles and made her look at the bones of Sister Janina. They even took her rosary and prayer book away.

The doctors observed that, as time progressed, Stella began to socialize with others. She also started eating again and resumed a relatively normal demeanor. As the extension time expired, the doctors released her, saying she was mentally competent.

The trial day arrived on the 13th of October. It would become Leelanau County's most sensational trial. The small Leland courthouse was packed every day, the crowd including many Felician nuns and priests. Some of the sisters had come from a distance and had taken their own scant money to pay for travel and lodging just to be there.

One of the first shocking revelations came with the testimony of a Wisconsin nun, Sister Mary Piuss, who confirmed that Bishop Kozlowski, who served at her parish, shared the knowledge of Sister Mary Janina's tragic death shortly before his own death. He did not specifically say Stella's name. He had, however, told her Sister Mary Janina had been hit over the head, killed and buried in the basement of Holy Rosary by a "prominent woman" in Isadore. The nun believed the only prominent woman he would refer to was Stella.

The bishop had even requested Sister Pius travel to Holy Rosary to see if such a grave existed. Although the nun did search the basement thoroughly, she did not see anything that looked like a grave. She did not, however, remove the boards against the wall, where the grave existed.

The bishop had heard of this crime from another priest at his parish. If this priest had indeed heard it during a confession and shared it with the bishop, it would represent an extremely unusual situation. Because of the sanctity of the confessional, it's an unheard-of transgression for a priest to reveal what a penitent confesses.

Other testimony followed, each one damaging Stella's reputation and reinforcing her dislike of Sister Janina. A former friend of Stella's, the wife of the church sexton, described Stella as an angry woman who was jealous of the young nun. Not only did Stella not like Sister Janina, she disliked all of the nuns at Holy Rosary. When pressed, the witness confirmed that Stella had called the nuns whores and Sister Janina a slut. The witness said Stella confided in her that the priest and doctor went into Sister Janina's room alone.

Another witness was called. She was an older Polish woman who claimed to have seen Stella shortly after the nun disappeared. According to her testimony, the housekeeper was very distraught, nervous. The witness claimed to have overheard Stella say, "Pray, Father, that they don't find her!"[2]

Perhaps one of the most dramatic moments occurred when the prosecution brought out the small box containing the remains of Sister Janina. Dr. Fralick slowly laid out the bones, creating the skeleton that was once Sister Mary Janina. The skeletal outline rested just a few feet from the housekeeper.

Weeping could be heard from some of the nuns in the courtroom. A few were seen with heads bowed, rocking in silent grief. Stella looked at the bones, her expression completely void of emotion.

During Dr. Fralick's testimony, he stated the facture on the skull was the victim's cause of death. A dark stain on the inside where the facture occurred was blood. This would prove the victim was alive at the time it was inflicted.

Next came testimony from the psychiatrist who treated Stella at the University of Michigan psychiatric ward. His detailed testimony concluded that Stella's psychiatric condition was faked.

The final surprise in the prosecution's case came when they called their last witnesses, Mary Tylicki, the undercover detective who had shared the housekeeper's cell for a few days. During that testimony, she swore the housekeeper had asked her to "… see Father Bieniawski and tell him to get Father Podlaszewski out of the States. He will pay you well. Tell him that Father Podlaszewski knows all."[3]

---

2 "The Mystery of the Missing Nun." *Wide World Magazine*, 1920, p. 230.
3 Ibid

The detective further testified that Stella had confessed to the whole thing. She had lured Sister Mary Janina to the basement cellar. When the nun arrived, the housekeeper hit and stunned the young, unsuspecting nun and went to get a shovel from the garden.

Stella returned and quickly dug a shallow grave, attempting to put Sister Janina in it, but the nun would not stay down. She hit Janina over the head with the back of the shovel. The nun's head still rose. Stella hit her head a second and third time. Finally, Sister Janina no longer moved. The housekeeper quickly pulled the dirt over the inert body and laid the heavy wooden boards over it. As if this could be any worse, Dr. Fralick confirmed Sister Janina was very likely alive when she was buried.

Mary's testimony continued. She said that Stella told her when the smell started she brought some of the pastor's chickens to the basement. Chickens, she claimed, always gave off a bad odor. She thought the chickens were a good cover for the smell of the decomposing body.

One of her final revelations was that Stella had told her she planned on acting insane to avoid prosecution. They couldn't prosecute someone not mentally competent.

Mary also shared the fact that Stella had confessed her sin to Father Francis Nowak, the Milwaukee priest serving at the same parish as Bishop Koslowski. This occurred during the time Stella was staying at her daughter's house in Wisconsin. Stella was relieved that she was now free of the sin she had committed in the eyes of God. If the undercover detective's testimony was true, then we finally know from whom the Bishop learned of the murder.

With the conclusion of Mary Tylicki's testimony, the prosecution rested. It was now the defense's turn.

The defense did not have many witnesses on their list. The first was a Polish-speaking woman who served as an interpretor during Stella's arrest in Manistee. She was going to testify about a blank document the Sheriff wanted Stella to sign, which would allow them to enter a confession after signature. She was also going to share that she had heard the arresting officers say they intended to get a confession out of Stella one way or another. Unfortunately, since Stella didn't sign the blank document and the prosecution didn't include the document as evidence, the judge dismissed the witness without testimony.

Defense then brought in a well-known physician who claimed the fracture on the skull occurred after death not before. He suggested the facture occurred from shovels coming down on the skull at the time the bones were discovered.

The prosecution attempted to dispute this on cross-examination, again referencing the dark stains around the fracture area. The physician claimed to not see the stains. In an interesting move, the prosecution had the skull brought to the jurors for their own evaluation. The physician finally concluded saying his evaluation was just his opinion.

It was at the end the defense brought in their most important witness, Stella. She swore that all the testimony brought forward by the prosecution witnesses were lies. She never said disparaging words about the nuns or Sister Mary Janina. She never struck or hurt any of the nuns and was not angry nor even concerned that Father Bieniawski spent a good deal of his time with Sister Janina. She was too busy with other work at the rectory to worry about what the priest did.

Stella also claimed to have known the woman brought into her cell was a spy and further swore she never confessed anything. Stella went on to tell of the cruel, abusive treatment she received under the hands the sheriff, detectives and the spy. The torture was so horrible that she was certain it had affected her physical and mental health permanently.

Throughout her testimony, Stella was stoic, firm, in control. It was during this final testimony, however, when Stella finally broke down. Deep, heart-wrenching sobs tore through her body as tears flowed. Was it an act or were the tears real? More importantly, did the jury believe her tears were real?

The faces of the jury members were inscrutable. Newspapers would say her testimony was powerful. Was it, however, enough to bring back a verdict of not guilty?

The trial concluded. Instructions were given to the jury of twelve men and deliberations began. Eight hours passed. Several ballots had been taken before a common verdict was reached. Finally, at 4:30 a.m., a verdict came. Guilty of Murder in the First Degree. Stella was sentenced to life in prison and sent to the Detroit House of Corrections.

The moment Stella began her life sentence at the Detroit House of Correction, Father Bieniawski gathered her attorneys to begin an appeal process and to continue his search for the real killer of Sister Janina. It seems he adamantly believed his housekeeper was not guilty of the crime.

He again, from his own pocket, paid for the attorneys to continue their work toward Stella's release. The appeal eventually failed and Father Bieniawski was unable to discover any new or different clues that might lead him to Janina's true murderer. Still, he did not give up. Seven years later, through his dedicated efforts, he managed to get her paroled. Stella was free.

What was Father Bieniawski's motivation? What caused him to spend so much of his money and time to fight for the release of a woman who had mercilessly killed and disrespectfully buried a Felician nun? Not just any nun, but a nun to whom the priest had become very close?

He must have truly believed his housekeeper was innocent. Either that or he felt extreme guilt thinking it was his sinful actions that had caused her to do such a monstrous thing. There is also the much more remote possibility he conspired with someone to end Janina's life while he was gone, giving him a clean alibi. He knew, if Sister Janina had been pregnant with his child, it would have ended his career aspirations in the Church. Whatever the situation, it was his work that eventually got Stella released.

Interestingly enough, after her release, Stella was hired by the Felician Order of Wisconsin to serve as their cook. There she remained for many years. Apparently, her health and mind not permanently affected as she once thought, she lived a full life of deep faith until her death in 1962. She was 92.

Now comes the never-ending belief Sister Mary Janina was pregnant. There is no clear-cut evidence that she was. There are those who claim

St. Isadore Cemetery. In background center is a large cross where the remains of Sister Mary Janina may be buried. (Roger Popa)

the small skeletal frame of a fetus was discovered with the body of Sister Janina but it was kept silent, suggesting yet another cover-up in this story.

The coroners performing the autopsy were the two local physicians, George Fralick and James Slepica. Dr. Fralick, of course, was the doctor who visited Sister Janina privately at least once a week. If he or Father Bieniawski (or both) were the lovers of Sister Janina or if Dr. Fralick's visits were related to prenatal care, he did not share that information nor were those types of questions posed to him or Father Bieniawski during their testimony.

Would Dr. Slepica have gone along with the cover-up? Possibly. Especially if he knew the father of the child was his associate, Dr. Fralick, or the priest. However, we have to consider how extremely delicate the small bones of a fetus are and take into account not all of Sister Janina's bones were found. The smaller bones of her feet, hands, and even a portion of rib were not recovered in the dark confines of the basement. It seems somewhat likely the same thing would have happened to the fine bones of a fetus.

That, of course, assumes Sister Janina was pregnant. There is no proof, no documentation, no statement that suggested this fact. The thought that she was pregnant is a guess. A guess isn't fact.

There are so many unanswered questions in this true story. What are the answers?

Could a short, diminutive-sized woman like Stella who stood under 5 ft. and weighed around 100 lbs. be able to commit such a crime? Could she have bludgeoned Sister Janina, dug a grave and placed relatively heavy boards over it and do it quickly enough so her absence wasn't noted? Then, after committing such a vile crime, continue baking bread as if nothing had happened?

Who was driving the carriage the nuns heard come by the convent the night Janina went missing? What was the driver's purpose?

The basement of the church had been searched many times. Had the stacked boards been there at the time? Had no one thought to remove them in their thorough searches?

Just as perplexing, what was seen and heard in the swamp during the numerous searches for Sister Janina…the sound of singing…Janina's favorite hymn…footprints that began and suddenly ended in the most remote sections of the swamp…the strange light that moved through the dense cedars…the dark figure seen heading toward the swamp late at night?

Poor little Josephine Mezek. What an incredibly difficult life she had. A young child growing up in the slums, experiencing the horror of her father's murder and the fear of seeing her mother fall into a dark world of insanity.

Josephine Mezek, a little girl torn from all that she knew, all that she loved at the tender age of nine and relocated to the cloistered life of the Felician Order. Yet even there she wasn't protected.

Why was life's burden so heavy on this woman? Could there be some sliver of truth to the old folklore that some residents on Bunker Street were cursed? Had little Josephine's fate been sealed back then?

It was like a dark cloud, a curse that followed her through life. Tuberculosis drove her slowly, inevitably toward her tragic end at Holy Rosary Church, and possible eternal damnation from a sinful relationship with the priest or doctor.

If she was with child, the sin was compounded. No matter how pious she might have been throughout her life, according to Catholic faith, a sin this grave without proper repentance would doom her soul to eternal hell. Even if she had repented, she was not given the Last Rites prior to death. The only hope to save her soul would be through God's mercy inspired by prayers. It was said her Felician sisters prayed daily for the soul of Sister Mary Janina. Was it enough?

Unfortunately, following the trial the small wooden box containing the remains of Sister Mary Janina went missing. Some believe it may have been re-interred under the large cross in the center of the Parish Cemetery. No one knows with certainty. There is no record of her burial. There is no tombstone or marker.

When Sister Mary Janina's remains were uncovered in 1918, the unexplained light in the swamp disappeared and the singing stopped. No one paid attention to the wooded area behind the church after that.

No one has observed that wooded area behind the church for decades. Perhaps the singing has returned and, for those who watch, the burning candle may again be seen moving through the cedars, the carrier of that light on a solitary journey.

What is the fate of Sister Mary Janina?

The Last Goodbye

Metro Detroit, MI

My sister, Kat, and I had conducted hundreds of investigations over an 11-year period. The majority were historic locations, some dating to the 18th century. Yet, here we were outside a very modern, two-story home not more than a few years old.[1] It was located in a nice suburban neighborhood north of Detroit. People passing would never suspect the home's owner was experiencing terrifying paranormal activity within its walls. Little did we know we were about to encounter our most unsettling residential case.

The call came on a late Wednesday evening near the end of February. Normally, Kat would have just let the answering service pick it up. For some reason on this cold evening, she answered.

It was a woman. Her name was Linda. Her strained voice and rapid blur of words spoke of her fear and confusion. She had gotten our name from a friend who had read our books and met us a few times. Her friend recommended she call us.

Linda told Kat she had contacted a paranormal team who were supposed to come a few months before but

---

1 *Because this story revolves around a private residential investigation, we have kept the identity of the location, individual's names and those involved confidential. We have changed names to retain their privacy and our promise of confidentiality.*

Photo Credit: Petra Gagilas; "Spiral" (taken January 5, 2014)

they never showed. She went on to explain that strange things had been happening at her home for several months but now something had just happened that sent her rushing away from home in her pajamas and slippers. She was taking safe haven at a friend's place until someone came to help her.

Kat promised we would meet her the next day. That is what brought us here.

There was a car in the drive that told us Linda and her friend, Brenda, were waiting for us. The front door swung open before we had a chance to ring the bell.

"I can't tell you how happy I am to see you!" Linda eagerly waved us inside.

We immediately noticed the inside of the home was as beautiful as the outside. The living room was well designed and meticulously clean. Like many proud parents and grandparents, she had family photographs everywhere.

Linda was a petite lady in her early fifties who couldn't seem to sit still and spoke in rapid, short sentences. Dark shadows rimmed her eyes, telling us she hadn't gotten much sleep the night before.

The first thing that needed to be done was calm her. We began with some light conversation until she seemed more relaxed. That's when we asked her to tell us what was going on. She stopped for a moment, took a deep breath and started.

"I don't want you to think I'm crazy. I think my family thinks I'm crazy; but I am not." Linda was completely baffled. Her tone was almost pleading. "I'm an educated woman. I don't believe in ghosts, yet I can't understand what is happening."

It started about a year ago. At first little, odd things would happen. Not terribly frightening but definitely unusual.

One evening a neighbor was over and they were chatting in her front room. She noticed her friend began staring at something then pointed across the room.

"Look at the lamp. The shade is turning." They turned their attention to a living room lamp. The lampshade spun quickly then shook and stopped. Linda went over to see what might be causing the movement. There were no air vents, fans or breezes. Definitely odd but they tossed it off and continued their conversation.

As the days and weeks passed odd things continued. Noises, thumps, bangs and the occasional sound of footsteps were heard when no one but Linda was in the house. She was familiar with the normal sounds her house made but these were different.

Linda pushed them off, trying to ignore them even when they became more frequent. Even the electricity began playing games. The lights in the house and even the TV were turning on and off as though to taunt her.

What frustrated Linda even more was the fact that when her children visited nothing happened. They thought she was just overreacting and it was just her imagination.

Time passed and the sounds became persistent. One evening Linda was talking to a friend on the phone. They were planning a surprise birthday party for another friend. She had just thought of the theme for the party when the room seemed to grow darker. Linda swore the walls felt as though they were closing in on her. It was incredibly still in the house. Linda sensed someone or something was with her.

She then heard a sound, two breaths almost like moans, warm against her ear. It was close. She jumped up, her eyes rapidly searching the room. There was nothing unusual. Her heart felt as though it would pound right out of her chest. Thankfully her friend's voice brought her back to reality.

"Are you okay?"

Linda's nervous response was, "Maybe I'm just a little on edge today."

A few weeks later another incident happened. She'd heard a voice, not much more than a quiet whisper. She turned in the direction of the sound and looked down the hall. That's when she first saw it. A fleeting glimpse of a solid, dark mass as it swiftly turned the corner of the hallway heading upstairs. It was shaped somewhat like a very tall person but without a definable head.

Linda couldn't take this any more. She needed help. That's when she contacted a paranormal team. They scheduled a time to come but they never showed.

She felt lost and helpless and didn't know whom to contact next so ended up doing nothing. She did her best to ignore the bumps, bangs and knocking that continued.

November came, bringing with it the anticipation of the holidays. Linda was in her kitchen alone preparing Thanksgiving dinner for the family who would be over in a few hours.

She wasn't thinking of much in particular, other than the chores that needed to be done before the family arrived, when she heard the voice again. This time it was clear, "Hi Mommy."

A shiver inched its way up her body and she felt a little lightheaded. Those two words had been whispered in her ear. It was a voice she recognized, her son Danny.

Linda stopped her story and looked at us with a nervous laugh. She crossed her arms tightly as if cold.

"My son Danny always called me Mommy even though he wasn't a child." It was his pet name for her. She hesitated a moment before telling us Danny had died a little over a year ago. She looked down, avoiding our gaze, "Maybe I am crazy."

We have been on many investigations. Her story up to this point wasn't that unusual. We calmed her down and offered words of assurance. We did our best to find out what was going on and encouraged her to continue. We didn't think she was crazy. She smiled, nodded and continued.

Her son Danny's death had happened a few days before Christmas a little over a year ago. He had been in a terrible accident on a snowy evening.

She walked over to a table, removed a picture frame and handed it to us. "That's Danny."

He was a good-looking young man in his early 30's. The photograph had him sitting on the beach with his girlfriend. A big, warm smile lit up his face with just a touch of wickedness in his eyes that suggested a man with a good sense of humor. He had a very deep tan, sandy hair and beard. You could sense the laughter spilling from his eyes.

Linda and Danny were very close. It was impossible for her to describe her feelings at this profound loss.

The weather had been horrible that night, she explained. Linda had begged Danny to spend the night but he laughed, "Mommy, you worry too much." A quick peck on the cheek and he headed out the door.

The fatal accident occurred just a few blocks from her house. Linda's worst fear had come true.

To make matters worse, just a couple of days before the accident she had received divorce papers from her husband of 35 years. Receiving those papers was traumatic and adding her son's death to her already fragile emotional state had almost put her over the edge. The next year was only bearable because of the support she received from her family and friends. Linda said she was really very fortunate and so grateful to them.

We sat quietly mesmerized and saddened by her tragic story. What a terrible burden to carry. Through all of this Linda kept her emotions in check, almost stoic, more than most people would have been able to do.

We asked if she was on any medications. She said yes, as she took a sip of wine, some type of tranquilizer.

We inwardly assessed the situation. With her current emotional state, coupled with medication and the occasional glass of wine, Linda could lose her sense of reality. At least that was something we would need to consider during this investigation.

Linda continued her story.

It seemed to come to a head two days ago. She had just come home from dinner with Brenda and had curled up in her favorite living room chair to watch TV. She recalled feeling very relaxed and wasn't upset or even sad at the time. It was then she heard the footsteps coming from the back rec room.

"It sounded like a gang of people broke into my home! I jumped off the chair." Her eyebrows pinched together and she briefly closed her eyes as if trying to block out the memory. There had been a few break-ins down the street. Her first thought was that someone had broken into her home.

"Who's there?" She had called out. There was no response. Instead, the sound of footsteps increased to something more like running. It continued to grow louder, like the deafening roar of a buffalo stampede. To Linda it felt like the very foundations of the home were shaking. The thunderous sounds were leaving the rec room and moving into the dinning room, then the kitchen. It was headed her way.

Shock and pure fear kept her locked in place for a moment. What the hell was going on? Then her mind and body went into survival mode. She grabbed her keys and phone, ran to the door, and slammed it behind her.

She was standing outside feeling a little safer, although her heart was still racing and the adrenaline in her body still exploding. It didn't take long, however, for her mind to clear enough to realize it was bitterly cold outside, she was just wearing pajamas and didn't have shoes or a coat.

Just then the phone in her hand rang. She jumped, fumbled with it for a moment and answered. It was the cheerful, upbeat voice of her son, "Hey mom what's up?" He was in California that evening but was expected home the next day.

Linda almost screamed in response. "There is someone or something in my house!"

She explained what had happened. He didn't seem to understand the seriousness of the situation. He asked if she saw who it was. When she said no, it was just a sound, he told her to settle down. He would be there tomorrow and check everything out. Linda's mind was racing—tomorrow isn't going to help tonight!

She told him she was going to Brenda's place to stay the night then proceeded to tell him she was standing outside freezing and in just pajamas. He encouraged her to go back inside and at least get a pair of shoes and a warm coat.

The phone with her son's voice coming through it was her momentary strength. Listening to his voice as he continued to tell her it would be okay, she slowly opened the front door and peered inside. The sound was no longer on the first floor but had moved upstairs. Going towards the kitchen and dining room, her hands flew to her face. She was not prepared for what she saw.

It was like a tornado had come through. Pictures on the walls were crooked. The formal dinning room table was a mess with the lace tablecloth bunched up in the center. Yet, strangely the candlesticks remained untouched. The chairs had been pulled out and were facing each other. Her sweater originally on the back of a chair was now in a pile on the floor.

This was like some horrible nightmare but it wasn't a dream. There was absolutely no explanation. She described everything she saw to her son as she headed toward the closet to get a coat, explaining she had to leave quickly in case whatever it was came downstairs again. Her eyes lifted to the second floor where she heard the noise moving from room to room. Was it searching for something or someone?

She didn't spend much time thinking about it at that moment. Her son kept reminding her that everything would be okay and he'd be home tomorrow. Linda, not wanting to worry him more than she already had, agreed with him. She told him she would be fine now and wished him a safe trip home before saying goodbye.

Linda focused on the task of quickly getting her coat and shoes. As she hurried down the hall, the phone rang again. It wasn't her son this time, but Brenda.

"Oh my goodness, Brenda, you won't believe what is going on!" she said as she slipped into her shoes and grabbed her coat.

Talking to Brenda gave her courage and, as she passed the basement door, she stopped. There was a small sound coming from below. She pulled up the rest of the courage she had and swung open the door, flipping on the lights.

Brenda heard Linda's quick intake of breath followed by silence. She urgently asked Linda what she saw. "Brenda, the ceiling tiles have been torn down. It looks like their metal moorings are twisted. There are still a few fiberboards hanging down from the ceiling and they're slowly swinging back and forth."

Terrified at what she saw, she turned the light out and slammed the door shut. Less than a second later, a loud noise riveted her in place. The sound was similar to a cherry bomb going off. Next came the knocks. Three solid raps from somewhere below followed by a moment of silence then three more raps. She counted four series of three raps. She didn't know why she was keeping count but she did.

Linda was telling Brenda about the knocks when the footsteps began. They were coming from the basement. Each footstep making a heavy thud on the stair as it ascended. Again not knowing why, she started counting … 6,7,8. They were moving closer to the door

She whispered to Brenda, "Heavy footsteps. They're coming upstairs."

Brenda shouted at her, "What are you doing? Get the hell out of the house!"

Needing no further prompt, Linda ran out of the house and directly into her car. She remembered how icy cold the car seats were but their coldness was comforting. She felt safe in the car. Not looking back at the house, Linda drove directly to Brenda's, where she stayed until shortly before we arrived.

Linda was nervously laughing as she concluded this bizarre story. She shook her head, "I left everything on in the house … all the lights, the TV … everything. I didn't even deadbolt the front door." She fell into silence, running a hand across her face as if to wipe out the memory.

Brenda looked at us, "I could see the terror in her eyes. I have never seen her look that way."

We asked if we could look around the house. Linda nodded, saying, "Of course. Wherever you want to go."

We wandered into the kitchen and dining room with Linda and Brenda close behind. This area had supposedly been a disaster the night before. It was now very neat and orderly. Picture frames balanced, tablecloth smoothly draped, and the eight heavy chairs in place. It looked nothing like Linda had described.

We looked at her with a question in our eyes. Her friend, Brenda, responded, "She couldn't stand looking at it so we tidied up before you arrived."

When asked if any photos had been taken of the way it had looked before, Linda shook her head. She hadn't thought of it. Of course, we had to consider the possibility the story may have been over embellished or not true.

Upstairs there were several bedrooms. One was her bedroom and the others were for her children or grandkids when they visited. The two ladies showed us Danny's room. Linda mentioned she had pretty much kept the room untouched from the way he had it.

We returned to the main floor and headed towards the basement. Linda hesitated, "If you don't mind, I'll stay up here."

"Sure, of course," I said. Then, with a smile, "We won't get lost."

Kat and I went down the hallway and opened the door. Okay. This was something.

Almost the entire ceiling had come down just as Linda had said.

We descended to the basement floor, carefully stepping around the fallen panels. Inspecting the torn metal bands that had once held the tiles in place, we noted they weren't cut but tightly twisted off. Someone or something had twisted each bracket away from the tiles.

Interesting. Both ladies were short and very petite. It would have been difficult for them to reach the tall ceiling and even more difficult for them to physically pry off all the tiles. Someone else could have done this but who and why? Her living son was in California and it just didn't seem logical her daughter, who lived in another city and was the mother of two young children, would do something like this. What were we dealing with?

Brenda needed help. That evening we weren't prepared for a long investigation but did spend a couple of hours running EVP[2] sessions throughout the house and basement. We would discover the next day that we had recorded one EVP.

Only one, but the EVP compelled us to return over and over. It was recorded moments after she finished the full story of her most terrifying night. She had been describing what the kitchen and dining room looked like when the voice came through. It was a male voice. Just three soft words, "I did it."

We looked at each other and knew there was something at Linda's house. We had to go back.

Our next trip to the house we played the recording for her. She listened intently. Her body suddenly stiffened. We knew she heard it.

---

2 EVP (electronic voice phenomena) Session. An EVP is believed to be the voice of a spirit. The sound is too low to be heard by ear but can be recorded on an audio recorder. Later, the audio file can be loaded into an audio editing software program and adjustments made to hear the voice. An EVP Session is a series of questions asked to elicit a response.

"I think it's my son." Linda turned away as tears glistened in the corners of her eyes. She quickly brushed them aside and looked at us, "Why would he do something like that?"

That is what we needed to find out. It could be her son but maybe not. There is a theory in the paranormal that negative entities or demons can mimic deceased loved ones to gain the confidence of an individual. It gives the entity more strength. The series of three knocks is often believed to be the sign of a demonic.

The three knocks mock the Holy Trinity. It is an unholy entity that wants to demean the holiness of the Trinity and offend God.

Of course a theory is just someone's guess. Theories in the paranormal community are rarely based on any scientific laws. The person who makes the theory up simply does so because it seems logical in their minds. Of course, what may seem logical to them may not actually be logical and it most certainly does not mean it's the truth.

At this point, we didn't want to scare Linda any more than she already was. We decided not to share this theory until we learned more.

Over the next few weeks, Linda returned to living in her home. There were sounds and bumps but nothing extreme. In fact, to some degree, the unusual sounds had lessened. During that time we also began a series of investigations.

Once or twice we spent the entire night in lockdown. Unfortunately, nothing was recorded or experienced, not even the slightest elevation in EMF (electro-magnetic field) levels.

The only one who heard anything during those weeks was Linda and only when at home alone. We wanted to get to the bottom of this.

The catalyst for activity seemed to be Linda alone in the house. Whatever was attempting to communicate wanted to communicate with her and no one else. That's when we decided to try a new approach.

For the night's investigation, Brenda was joined by another friend, Bill. After greetings, we asked Linda do exactly what she would normally do when she was alone. She nodded, took off her shoes, sat in her favorite chair, wrapped herself in an afghan and turned on TV. The only deviation was that we asked she turn off the sound.

We left an audio recorder and EMF meter with her and set up a video recorder across the room. Kat asked her to start talking as she might if her son, family member or a friend was there.

While she began, the rest of us retreated to the dining room. We sat very still for the next few hours. Off and on we would hear Linda talking and asking questions. For the first time in our past investigation, the EMF meter next to Linda began getting hits.

Eventually, our group joined Linda to continue the investigation. The EMF meter continued recording elevations every time Danny's name was mentioned. Kat and I were encouraged.

The next morning we started the review of audio and video. This time we were getting somewhere. EVPs had been captured. All occurred when Linda was sitting alone. The first clip was a male voice. It asked, "Where's Crystal?"

We had no idea who Crystal was and if it was relevant to the activity. There were other EVPs, some clear and others not but all sounded like the same voice.

The most significant EVP was the one that spoke directly to Linda. She just asked if Danny was near. The whispered reply was quiet but clear, "Hi mommy, it's me, I love you. "

Linda sounded relieved when we called telling her we had captured some audio evidence. We scheduled a time to go over it.

During our evidence review she had a number of family and friends over. They were gathered around the dining room table eager to hear what had been captured.

The first EVP we shared was "Where is Crystal?" As soon as the words came over the speaker, we noticed the startled look on several faces. Linda instantly jumped up, "Oh my goodness, that's Danny's dog! He loved his little shelter dog."

She explained that when he would go away for business or vacation she took care of Crystal. "Dan would always call to check on his little dog." Linda continued, "Crystal stayed with me after his death but with my work schedule I just wasn't here enough so my daughter took her.

Linda laughed and looked up in the air, "She's fine, Danny, and with your sister."

We presented our other EVPs. The voices were very similar, male and according to Linda sounded like her son. "I knew he was here."

We saved the most important audio clip for last. When we first heard it at the office it left us speechless. We played the last clip. "Hi mommy, it's me. I love you."

There was a solemn silence. No one said a word. A few stared at their hands as they wiped away stray tears. Linda looked unusually calm, almost serene.

"That's my Danny. He just wanted me to know." She again looked toward the heavens, "I love you, too, baby."

What followed for the rest of the evening was almost a celebration. Food was ordered – lots of food. Everyone ate as though they were starving; their solemn mood had now lifted.

Linda felt vindicated. She wasn't crazy. Most importantly, Linda heard from her son, and she had heard what she wanted to hear for more than a year.

It's investigations like this that make us happy to do what we do. A follow-up call was made to Linda about a month later. She was cheerful and upbeat. Everything was calm. Things were going well.

There was, however, one thing she mentioned which put up a caution sign. Her daughter had recently spent the night. The next morning she took a shower in the upstairs bathroom. Once out of the shower, the room filled with steam, she noticed something unusual in the mirror and called her mother up to check it out.

According to Linda it was a series of circles connected to each other. "It looked like this crazy spiral."

After Linda recounted the event, we asked her not to touch the mirror and said we'd be over in the next couple of days. She promised she wouldn't touch the mirror. However, she was having family over for Easter and didn't want to get together until after that. It was left that she would call sometime after Easter.

We heard nothing. Then one day in May she called. Her voice was urgent.

"This couldn't happen at a worse time! I am leaving with my friends for a two-week vacation tomorrow and think things are acting up in my house again."

As she explained, she had just come back from dinner with Brenda. They were sitting in the car, parked in her driveway and talking about the next morning's trip.

She explained that before leaving for dinner that evening, she left the lights on in the front room and closed the sheers across the large bay window. While chatting in the car, something caught their eye in the window.

Through the thin veil of the sheers, she and Brenda saw a form moving through her front room. It was dense enough to cast a shadow across her drapes.

We asked if it looked like a man wandering around her house. "Well something was in the house. It wasn't a man." She replied. "It's much bulkier and from what I could tell, didn't have a head."

She continued, "It passed through the front room window, disappeared behind the wall and then reappeared in the narrow window of the front door. It was completely black, and for a moment, blocked out the light. Then we could see it turn and head upstairs."

The story didn't end there.

"The horrible part was, as one mass went upstairs, we saw another walking through the front room. It followed the same path as the first. Not long after a third mass moved through."

Kat and I looked at one another. There was the number three again, the theory associated with a sign of a demonic.

We told her we would come right over. She said no. She would stay at Brenda's house tonight. However, she needed the courage to go in and get her suitcase and asked us to stay on the phone while she did that.

We talked to her, offering words of encouragement as she headed toward the house. Linda's deep breath rasped through the phone's speaker as we heard her place and turn the key in the door and open it. The sound of Brenda's halted whispers told us she was close behind.

A second or two passed in silence, then Linda's voice, tight and tense, came through the phone. "Everything seems fine. I don't feel anything unusual."

We could hear her and Brenda quietly talking to each other as they walked through the house. Her voice was a little more confident this time, "Everything looks in order. Nothing is out of place."

Kat and I heard her take another deep breath, then a sigh followed by a nervous chuckle. "Oh Lord, now I have to go upstairs to get my luggage."

In the background we heard her Brenda whisper, "Jesus, Linda, let's just get it and get out of here!"

Linda's rapid breath rasped through the phone as she walked to the second floor. Footsteps told us Brenda was right behind her. At the top of the stairs they halted. More silence.

Linda whispered, 'Everything seems fine. We're going down the hall to get my luggage." The sound of soft footsteps came through the phone as they padded through the hall.

"I've reached my bedroom and we're going in," Linda again whispered. "I'm putting the phone down but don't hang up!"

We heard the two women fumbling with luggage and, in the background, the frustrated voice of Brenda, "Did you have to bring so much?"

"Well, I've got stuff I have to bring. We can get this in one trip!"

More fumbling of luggage and something that may have been a curse came from Brenda. A few seconds passed before Linda again picked up phone. "OK, we're leaving."

This time rapid footsteps were heard as the ladies moved quickly down the hall. Then Linda stopped. Brenda's frustrated voice, "Oh for heaven's sake! Why did you stop?

"Yes," I said. "Why did you stop?"

"We're right outside the bathroom. I want to check the circles in the mirror."

We told her it was a good idea and waited. Again, her whispered voice was heard. "The spiral thing has changed. I think it started changing, getting harder to see last week. It had changed from a spiral to more disconnected circles. Now, I don't see it at all."

In the background was Brenda's frustrated voice, "Great. It's gone. Can we go now?"

Moments later they were outside, relief in their voices as they retold the experience. I asked her to call us if she needed our help after the vacation. Linda promised she would.

This case was investigated a few years back. It's one we still talk about and always will. Several unanswered questions have resulted in considerable lack of sleep. What was going on at Linda's home? Several possibilities taunt us today.

There is another one of those theories in the paranormal community that would apply to Linda's case. The kind of activity where loud sounds occur and objects are moved or thrown are called poltergeist (the name poltergeist being of Germanic origin meaning active ghost.)

The belief is that people experiencing severe depression or any extreme emotion can create poltergeist activity. Their own stirred-up emotions generating a form of negative energy that can be destructive. Yet another theory suggests those dealing with depression may attract demons or evil spirits.

Did Linda, unknowingly, create the extreme activity from her own ravaged emotions or had she drawn something negative to her? The three knocks repeated several times in the basement on that first night and the three dark masses moving upstairs on the last day represent the pattern of the unholy trinity.

Of course, if we believe this theory, the EVPs Linda believed were her son's voice were not. It was a trick by the evil entity disguising itself in Danny's voice to draw her closer in order to take control.

The other possibility and one that Kat and I believe is what likely happened is that Linda's profound grief along with her fixation on hearing from Danny may have drawn her son to her from the other side. To communicate, a portal was formed. This would explain the spiral (vortex) seen in the upstairs bathroom.

This portal allowed not only her son's spirit to slip through but something else – something darker. An entity that is unknown in this dimension.

When Danny couldn't get his mother to respond to his attempts at communication, he became frustrated and made more of an effort to get her attention … the twirling lamp shade and the voice, "Hi, Mommy" heard around Thanksgiving.

When that didn't' work, the other entities that came through with Danny took over and went too far. Although they did not hurt Linda in any way, they did create the terrifying event that eventually led Linda to us. An action that finally allowed Linda to hear Danny's last goodbye.

After that, Danny re-entered the vortex. Then he realized the dark entities had been left behind and returned to call them back.

That may have been what Linda and Brenda saw the night before their trip. The three dark entities heading upstairs were being summoned to return. Once they entered, Danny closed the gateway protecting his mother and family from whatever damage they may have done. The spiral was now gone. The gateway closed. The home was clean, safe.

When Linda returned from vacation, the home was quiet. She didn't hear directly from her son again but was okay with that. His last message was enough to lift a heavy weight from her heart. Danny was with her. She was certain of it now. He still watched over her and, most importantly, she knew wherever he was their love continued.

Tribute to my sister, co-author and best friend
Beverlee J. Rydel

(Photo by Julie Welch)

As my sister always said, she was my big sister "since birth." She had an incredible wit (often sarcastic) and easily laughed.

We were best friends always. She was there supporting me throughout my life—first date—first job interview—first failure. She was Maid of Honor at my wedding and kept me calm through those wedding day jitters. She pulled me out of the very dark place I was in after my husband's sudden death. Although she didn't know it, she saved my life then.

Truthfully, there is nothing she would not have done for me. There is nothing I would not have done for her. I was blessed to have her as my sister. I am blessed to have known her.

Professionally, Bev served as Vice President of Human Resources for several banks including First of America. In the mid-1990's she left her corporate life to join me in a new adventure—our own business.

Although she continued as an independent consultant in human resources, we started writing books. It was actually a family venture because my mother, Clara, and my husband, Chris, Bev and I became a team.

The first in our book series was the *Michigan Vacation Guide*. There were seven books in that series. It did very well and, according to the Barnes and Noble regional sales manager, was in the top five best-selling Michigan travel books. It was placed on the Secretary of State's Read Michigan list in 1995.

With the passing of our mother, we lost interest in the series and went on a writing hiatus for a while. Then one evening Bev, Chris, and I went to dinner at a wonderful restaurant in Detroit, Michigan called The Whitney. Unknown to us at the time, that trip would prove to be the catalyst for our next book series with a photo Bev took which we were never able to explain.

Our curiosity to find an explanation took us on an 11-year paranormal journey. My sister and I would sometimes travel more than 10,000 miles a year searching out and investigating reports of unexplained phenomena. My husband would laugh and call us Thelma and Louise of the Paranormal. Give us a car with a tank of gas, and we were ready for the next trip.

Of the hundreds of investigations conducted, we found about 35 to 40 cases that were unexplainable. Most of those cases were included in our *Haunted Travels of Michigan* book trilogy. That series now represents our most haunted Michigan adventures.

In September 2012, Bev was diagnosed with advance-stage cancer. Though her life expectancy was less than 12 months, she was determined to beat the odds. She fought through the multiple surgeries, multiple chemo and radiation treatments with humor, incredible bravery and grace for three years. During those three years she lived life to the fullest.

We continued our paranormal adventures but also took time for other things. A cross-country train trip from Michigan to New Mexico followed by a week exploring historic towns, petroglyphs and Mayan ruins. Then another trip to the Mammoth Caves and smaller road trips to visit friends or see sites closer to home.

Our last adventure would check off more things from Bev's bucket list. This would be a very special paranormal road trip. The first stop would take us to the Jailer's Inn in Bardstown, Kentucky. Although no ghosts were found at the inn, we did find some spirits at the historic bourbon bar next door. That's where we discovered the awesomeness of cherry bourbon.

Then on to St. Francisville, Louisiana for a two-night stay at the Myrtles Plantation. This is considered one of America's most haunted locations and a place Bev had wanted to visit for many years. More friends joined us to share in our investigation of the Myrtles. What a memorable time we had. Again, we didn't turn up any paranormal evidence but were not disappointed. It was an amazing opportunity for us to stay at this historic location.

Besides investigating the plantation, we went on an airboat ride in the bayou. Bev held a baby alligator in her hands. More check marks on her bucket list. She laughed and was awed by the beautiful sights on that bayou trip. For the moment, she forgot about what lay ahead.

We left the Myrtles and headed to another plantation in Cheneyville, Louisiana called Lloyd Hall. A massive storm hit that night which blew over a huge old oak tree just behind us. Again, no ghostly activity was identified but that powerful storm was very impressive.

On our long drive back home, we stopped in Alabama and spent two nights at a beautiful beachfront hotel directly overlooking the Gulf of

Mexico. We went to sleep each night and woke each morning to the sound of rolling waves and ate breakfast on the balcony as we watched the waves crash to shore. My sister and I walked along the sandy beach and felt the sun on our face. It would be our last adventure together and, as Bev would later tell me, was her most favorite trip—ever.

(Photo by Diane Williams Shaw)

I will always remember one of the last words my sister said to me. We were in the hospital. She was nearing her end. I held her and asked if she were afraid.

"No," she whispered, "because you're here."

I was privileged to have Bev as my sister and my best friend. I was honored to be there with her—for her—until the very end.

Thank you big sister—for everything. This book is for you. I'll see you, Chris, mom and dad on the other side. I'll bring some cherry bourbon.

Bibliography

Chapter 1: Eloise Psychiatric Hospital

"Asylum Is Overcrowded: County Can Take No More Violently Insane at Eloise." *Detroit Free Press* 9 July 1909: 5.

"End of the Line for Eloise." *Detroit Free Press* 27 Sept. 1984: 7A.

Fburns@mlive.com, Gus Burns |. "Work Begins to Uncover Mystery of Westland's Eloise Cemetery." *MLive.com*. MLive.com, 12 Feb. 2016, http://www.mlive.com/news/detroit/index.ssf/2015/12/volunteers_work_to_reveal_myst.html

Felton, Ryan. "The Horror of Eloise Hospital: Haunted Michigan Mental Asylum Goes up for Sale." *The Guardian*. Guardian News and Media, 11 Nov. 2015, https://www.theguardian.com/us-news/2015/nov/11/eloise-hospital-haunted-michigan-mental-asylum

Hurd, Henry M., William F. Drewry, Richard Dewey, Charles W. Pilgrim, G. Alder Blumer, and T.J.S. Burgess. *The Institutional Care of the Insane in the United States and Canada*. Ed. Henry M. Hurd. Baltimore: Johns Hopkins, 1916.

Ibbotson, Patricia. *Eloise: Poorhouse, Farm, Asylum, and Hospital, 1839-1984*. Mt. Pleasant, South Carolina: Arcadia Publishing, 2002.

Keenan, Stanislas M. *History of Eloise: Wayne County Poorhouse*. Detroit: Thomas Smith, 1913.

"Reasons for Admission." Log Book 1864-1889. West Virginia's Hospital for the Insane.

Chapter 2: The Night Visitor

Brooks, Alexis. *Shadow People—Rosemary Ellen Guiley*. www.youtube.com/watch?v=e-3Plozi3X4.

Matthews, Dana. "The 'Shadow Man' Phenomena and the Terrifying 'Hat Man' Visitations." *Week In Weird*, 21 Nov. 2016, weekinweird.com/2016/08/31/investigating-the-link-between-the-shadow-man-phenomenon-and-the-terrifying-hat-man/.

Schwarz, Rob. "The 'Hat Man.'" *Stranger Dimensions*, 16 July 2017, www.strangerdimensions.com/2011/10/28/the-hat-man/.

Chapter 3: Spirit Painter

Adams, Joan. "To Her No Mystery." *Philadelphia Inquirer* 31 Mar. 1948: 139.

"Bush in Reno, Divorce Hinted in 2d Venture: To Wed Marian Spore, Artist and Charity Angel, Report Says." *Brooklyn Daily Eagle* 26 Feb. 1930: 1.

Bush, Marian Spore. *They.* New York: Beechhurst, 1947.

Dorman, Marjorie. "'Message from Dead' Depicted on Canvas Attracts Large Throng." *Brooklyn Daily Eagle* 3 Dec. 1924: 24.

"Ghosts Guide the Hand that Makes These Pictures." *Montgomery Advertiser* 23 July 1922: 2.

"Ghosts Your Best Friends, Is Most Recent Theory Advanced by Greenwich Village Artist." *Times Herald [Port Huron]* 14 Sept. 1923: 14.

"Is This Girl Painter Fake or Psychic?" *Brooklyn Daily Eagle* 23 Nov. 1934: 82.

"Leon Dabo Pays Tribute to Art of Marian Spore; Unable to Understand It." *Brooklyn Daily Eagle* 29 Oct. 1927: 27.

"Prophetess." *Time,* 7 June 1943, pp. 71-72.

"Says Hunches, Not Spirits Guide Brush." *Brooklyn Daily Eagle* 31 Jan. 1933: 1+.

"Spirit Paintings Shown." *New York Times* n.d.: 23.

Wilcox, Uthai Vincent. "Ghosts Guide Her Hand When She Paints." *Boston Sunday Post* 30 Oct. 1927, Feature sec.: n. pag.

Chapter 4: Direct Voice Medium

"The Alleged Exposure of Mrs. Wreidt." *The Light: A Journal of Psychical, Occult, and Mystical Research* 42.1652 (n.d.): 424.

Doyle, Arthur Conan. *The History of Spiritualism. Vol. II.* New York: George H. Duran, 1926.

Fanthorpe, Lionel, and Patricia Fanthorpe. *Mysteries and Secrets: The 16-Book Complete Codex.* Toronto: Dundurn, 2014.

Gauld, Alan. *Mediumship and Survival: A Century of Investigations.* New York: F+W Media, 2012.

Jago, Lucy. *The Northern Lights.* New York: Knopf Doubleday Group, 2001.

King, John Sumpter. *Dawn of the Awakened Mind*. N.p.: James A. McCann, 1920.

Leonard, Maurice. *People from the Other Side: The Enigmatic Fox Sisters and the History of Victorian Spiritualism*. Mt. Pleasant, South Carolina: The History Press, 2008.

Moore, W. Usborne, and Harry Price. *Spirit Identity by the Direct Voice: Striking Evidences of the Survival of Death*. London: Two Worlds, 1919.

Moore, William Usborne. *The Voices*. N.p.: White Crow, 2011.

Chapter 5: House of Funerals

"2 More Held in 10 Deaths." *Detroit Free Press* 28 Aug. 1931: 4.

Ashenfelter, David. "Detroit Had a Corruption Scandal in 1930s That Was Bigger Than Today's." – *Deadline Detroit*. Deadline Detroit Politics, 12 Feb. 2013. Web.

Brown, Vera. "Murder Suspect Is Feared by Witnessess." *Tyrone Daily Herald [Tyrone, PA]* 27 Aug. 1931: 1.

Brown, Vera. "Witch Lady Prisoner in Detroit Jail." *Shamokin News-Dispatch [Shamokin, PA]* 28 Aug. 1931:6.

"Criminal Charges Cap Their Careers as Law Officers." *Detroit Free Press* 22 Feb. 1940: 1.

"Delray Witch Gets Retrial." *Detroit Free Press* 17 Apr. 1945: 9.

"Free Veres Witnesses." *Detroit Free Press* 13 Sept. 1931: 13.

"Heart Attack Fatal to Duncan McCrea." *Detroit Free Press* 26 May 1951: 15.

"Hold Veres Witnesses: Investigators Detain One-Armed Man, Former Roomer." *Detroit Free Press* 3 Sept. 1931: 4.

"Iron Bludgeon Found Hidden in Veres Home." *Detroit Free Press* 29 Aug. 1931: 2.

"McCrea's Career a Storied One." *Detroit Free Press* 22 Feb. 1940: 1.

"Mrs. Veres and Son Arraigned." *Detroit Free Press* 1 Sept. 1931: 30.

"Mrs. Veres, Son Guilty." *Detroit Free Press* 6 Oct. 1931: 1.

"Neighbors Seek New Veres Trial." *Detroit Free Press* 7 Oct. 1931: 7.

"Nemesis of Detroit Witch Dies Blaming Her Evil Eye." *Detroit Free Press.* 9 May 1933: 1.

"New-Found Letter Adds to Complexity of Mystery." *Detroit Free Press* 30 Aug. 1931: 2.

"No Way Out for the Killing Witch." *The American Weekly* 18 Feb. 1945.

"Police Probe Mystery Death of Ten: Mother and Son Held." *Detroit Free Press* 27 Aug. 1931: 24.

"Spell of 'Evil Eye' Casts Gloom over Medina Street." *Detroit Free Press* 30 Aug. 1931: 2.

Tedsen, Kathleen. "Interview wih Annie Rusell, Jacob, Denise Porcelli, Beth Whiting, Janet White, Thomas White, and Jessica Gutowski." 14 Feb. 2015.

Tedsen, Kathleen. "Interview with Angel Balsdon, Krista Laughlin, and Tracy Muller." 15 Feb. 2015.

Tedsen, Kathleen. "Interview with Jody Debiew-Sooy." 16 Feb. 2015.

"They Called Her a Witch—It Cost Her 14 Years." *Detroit Free Press* 12 July 1959: 23.

"Veres Pair Given Life." *Detroit Free Press* 15 Oct. 1931: 1.

"Widow Confesses: Mrs. Veres and Son Held Without Bail as Slayers." *Detroit Free Press* 1 Sept. 1931: 1.

"[William] Veres Granted Freedom in 'Witch of Delray." *Detroit Free Press* 14 June 1944: n. pag.

"Witch Widow of Detroit Says She Killed One." *The Coshocton Tribune [Coshocton, OH]* 31 Aug. 1931: 8.

"Woman Held for Murder: 10 Men Missing." *Detroit Free Press* 26 Aug. 1931: 1.

Chapter 6: Eternal Retribution of the Sauk

Ellis, Franklin. *History of Shiawasee and Clinton Counties, Michigan.* Philadelphia: D.W. Ensign, 1880.

History of Bay County, Michigan. Chicago: H.R. Page, 1883.

Lawler, Joe. "Bones Found at Stone Street Development." *Flint Journal* 5 Dec. 2008: n. pag.

Leeson, M. A. *History of Macomb County, Michigan: Containing an Account of Its Settlement, Growth, Development and Resources, an Extensive and Minute Sketch of Its Cities, Towns and Villages, Their Improvements, Industries, Manufactories, Churches, Schools and Societies, Its War Record, Biographical Sketches, Portraits of Prominent Men and Early Settlers: The Whole Preceded by a History of Michigan, Statistics of the State and an Abstract of Its Laws and Constitution and of the Constitution of the United States.* Chicago: M.A. Leeson, 1882.

Chapter 7: Lost Boy of Mackinac Island

"The Mystery at Fairy Rock." *Jackson Citizen Patriot* 23 Oct. 1877: 4.

O'Brien, Frank A. *Names of Places of Interest on Mackinac Island, Michigan, Established, Designated, and Adopted by the Mackinac Island State Park Commission and the Michigan Historical Commission.* N.p.: Wynkoop, Hallenbeck, Crawford, State Printer, 1916.

Chapter 8: Murder House

"A Butchery." *Bay City Times* 28 Dec. 1889: 1.

"A Murderous Maniac." *The Jackson Citizen Patriot* 30 Dec. 1889: 1.

"A Young Woman at Mt. Vernon Hangs Herself." *Detroit Free Press* 8 Oct. 1874: 1.

"Child Plays with Copperhead." *The Indianapolis News* 3 June 1874: 2.

"The Horrible Deed of a Human Fiend Near Rochester, Mich." *The Bay City Times* 28 Dec. 1889: 1.

"Murder and Suicide: A Maniac's Terrible Deed—Killed Three Persons and Then Suicided." *Saginaw Evening News* 30 Dec. 1889: 1.

"Murder and Suicide: A Mt. Vernon Farmer Shoots His Wife, Daughter and Granddaughter." *Detroit Free Press* 29 Dec. 1889: 7.

"Slain in Their Sleep." *Kalamazoo Gazette* 29 Dec. 1889: 2.

"Triple Murder in Michigan." *Murder by Gaslight*, 14 Mar. 2015, gaslight56.rssing.com/browser.php?indx=7886490&item=143.

"W. Major's Bloody Work." *New York Times* 29 Dec. 1889: 6.

Woolever, Stewart J. A., Jr. "Biography of William R. Major, Warren, New Jersey." *USGen Web Archives - Census Wills Deeds Genealogy.* N.p., 2002.

Chapter 9: The Fate of Sister Mary Janina

"Bill Kettle and His Bloodhound Unravel Many Michigan Mysteries." *Detroit Free Press* 20 Oct. 1907: 8.

"Body of Woman Dug Up To Solve Mystery of Nun." *The Denver Post* 24 Feb. 1919: 73.

"Cannot Find Missing Nun." *Detroit Free Press* 28 Aug. 1907: 6.

"Committed to Asylum." *The Inter-Ocean [Chicago, IL]* 18 May 1883: 6.

"The Confession, Nun Case Plea: Defendant Testifies Woman Detective Beat Her in Leelanau Jail." *Detroit Free Press* 23 Oct. 1919: 15.

"Heard Weird Song But Watchers Fail To Find the Missing Isadore Nun." *Grand Rapids Press* 5 Sept. 1907: 5.

Link, Mardi. *Isadore's Secret: Sin, Murder, and Confession in a Northern Michigan Town.* Ann Arbor: U of Michigan, 2010.

"Mrs. Lypschinaki Found Guilty of Murdering Nun." *Battle Creek Enquirer* 25 Oct. 1919: 1.

"Murder in His Heart: Joseph Messik's Horrible Crime." *Chicago Herald* 1 Dec. 1890: 3.

"Murdered Nun's Ghost Said To Haunt U.S. Town." *The Winnipeg Tribune [Winnipeg, Canada]* 4 Apr. 1919: 9.

"Nun Case Nears Trial at Leland." *Detroit Free Press* 9 Oct. 1919: 8.

"Nun Murdered Is Assertion of Young Girl." *The Daily Times News [Ann Arbor, MI]* 24 Feb. 1919: 1.

"Nun Was Slain, Bishop's Word." *Detroit Free Press* 16 Oct. 1919: 1.

"Officer Soergi's Shot." *The Inter-Ocean [Chicago, IL]* 17 Jan. 1883: 8.

"Parish Will Join Search." *Flint Journal* 30 Aug. 1907: 5.

Polacheck, Hilda. *[The Dybbuk of Bunker Street].* Chicago, Illinois, 1939. Man uscript/Mixed Material. Retrieved from the Library of Con gress, <https://www.loc.gov/item/wpalh000080/>.

"Priest Killed Nun." *Detroit Free Press* 1 Mar. 1919: 2.

"Reward for Missing Nun." *Detroit Free Press* 10 Sept. 1907: 2.

"Says Bishop Knew That Nun Was Murdered." *The News-Palladium [Benton Harbor, MI]* 16 Oct. 1919: 1.

"Says Nun Is Safe: Priest Receives Mysterious Letter from Chicago." *The Flint Journal* 5 Oct. 1907: 8.

"She May Be Insane: Kidnapping Theory Regarding Missing Nun Is Discredited." *Grand Rapids Press* 27 Aug. 1907, Special to the Evening Press ed.: 9.

"Sister Mary Still Alive." *Detroit Free Press* 7 Sept. 1907: 8.

"State Depends on Daughter to Convict Mother of Nun Murder." *The Pittsburg Press* 3 Mar. 1919: 7.

"The Mystery of the Missing Nun." *Wide World Magazine,* 1920, p. 230.

"Third Time Downpour Prevents Success: Kingsley Clairvoyant Goes In a Trance and Says Missing Nun from Isadore Convent Was Abducted and Is Held Prisoner." *Detroit Free Press* 11 Sept. 1907: 7.

"Woman Confesses to Murder of Nun." *Lincoln Journal Star [Lincoln, NE]* 18 Oct. 1919: 2.

"Woman Jailed as Nun Killer." *Detroit Free Press* 30 Mar. 1919: 1.

Wright, Carroll D. *Seventh Special Report: The Slums of Baltimore, Chicago, New York and Philadelphia.* Washington, D.C.: Government Printing Office, 1894.